Listening to Music

History Age 9+

Compiled and written by Helen MacGregor

Illustrations by Alison Dexter

Produced in association with

hyperion

A & C Black · London

Contents

c800 *Medieval*

Introduction to the period   *page 4*

Columba aspexit   6

12th century devotional song by Hildegard of Bingen with activities exploring the early notation of pitch.

Estampie royal   10

Lively 12th century dance by an unknown composer; activities for investigating the structure then performing the piece on percussion.

Eno sagrado en Vigo • Aj ondas que eu vin veer   12

Two lyrical love songs by the 14th century troubadour, Martin Codax with song writing activities exploring mood.

Listening links   14
O viridissima virga

Devotional song by Hildegard of Bingen.

Danse royale

13th century stately court dance.

Onques n'amai tant que jou fui amee

A 13th century lament by a French troubadour, Richart de Fournival.

c1400

c1400 *Renaissance*

Introduction to the period   16

Pueri concinite   18

A religious song of celebration on the birth of Christ written by Jacob Handl in Italian style during the late 16th century. Activities exploring texture.

Martin said to his man   22

Nonsensical tavern song published by Thomas Ravenscroft in 1609. Activities in singing and creating new verses.

c1600

Mistress Winter's jump   24

Energetic Tudor dance by John Dowland. Dance activity based on authentic steps.

Listening links   26
Packington's pound

A popular Elizabethan tune arranged for street musicians.

In nomine

Mid 16th century piece of chamber organ music written by Richard Alwood for court entertainment.

Suzanna

A lilting dance played by a consort of lutes.

c1600 *Baroque*

Introduction to the period   28

Chiacona   30

Mid 17th century Italian music for cornetts, bass sackbut and harpsichord by Tarquinio Merula. Activities in performance and improvisation using a ground bass.

c1750 Sonata for harpsichord   34

One of Domenico Scarlatti's 555 sonatas written in the mid-18th century. Composition activities explore binary and ternary structure using domino cards.

Second movement from Recorder concerto   36

Early 18th century music for recorder and small orchestra by Antonio Vivaldi. Dance activities highlight the role of the recorder and accompanying instruments.

Listening links   38
Canzona super entrada aechiopicam

German music for cornetts and sackbuts by Samuel Scheidt.

Recorder concerto

First and last movements (see above).

The hunt cantata (chorus)

Music for voices and instruments by J S Bach.

Classical

c1750

c1820

Introduction to the period *40*

The 'hen' symphony *42*

Late 18th century orchestral music by Joseph Haydn. A vocal chant activity demonstrates the structure of the first movement and leads into composition.

A Christmas carol *46*

Late 18th century non conformist parish church music for voices. The children sing the carol with a simple instrumental bass accompaniment.

Ein Mädchen oder Weibchen *48*

An aria from Mozart's opera of 1791, *The magic flute*. A singing activity is combined with composing and performing an accompaniment.

Listening links *50*

The 'hen' symphony

Second movement (see above).

Pastorale

Orchestral music by Pieter Hellendaal in pastoral style.

Variations on Ein Mädchen oder Weibchen

Beethoven's arrangement of the aria for cello and piano.

Romantic

c1820

c1900

Introduction to the period *52*

Theme and variations from The 'trout' quintet *54*

Early 19th century chamber music by Franz Schubert. Activities in reading and writing a graphic score.

Polka *58*

Mid 19th century piano duet music by Alexander Borodin. Activities in playing a simple ostinato and composing melodies.

Waltz from Serenade for strings *60*

A movement from Peter Tchaikovsky's late 19th century orchestral music, *Serenade for strings*. Activities in composing a musical picture.

Listening links *62*

Scherzo

From The 'trout' quintet (see above).

Le rossignol

Piano music by Franz Liszt.

Sursum corda

Ceremonial orchestral music by Edward Elgar.

20th century

c1890

2000

Introduction to the period *64*

Gnossienne no 3 *66*

Turn of the century French impressionist piano music by Erik Satie in a transcription for orchestra. Activities using unusual scales and chords.

Fanfare for the common man *70*

Mid 20th century North American music for brass and percussion written by Aaron Copland in tribute to the allied troops of World War II. Activities in performing then composing a fanfare and in reading a graphic score.

Sextet *72*

A movement from Eleanor Alberga's contemporary dance music, *Dancing with the shadow* (1990). Activities in composing music with a similar structure of fast and slow sections.

Listening links *74*

La nuit

Ballet music by Satie.

Konzertmusik

German music for brass and strings by Paul Hindemith.

Paris fanfare

Ceremonial fanfare by Paul Patterson for the opening of the Channel Tunnel.

Medieval

c800–c1400

When Christianity spread across Europe after the fall of the Roman Empire in 410 AD, monasteries became centres for composing and performing music. Religious services often included dancing, singing and playing instruments.

Columba aspexit
by Hildegard of Bingen

This is a devotional song. It is a setting of religious prose which displays a more free and expressive style of singing than in plainchant. The monastic community performed music such as this as well as its large repertoire of plainchants.

A tradition of singing simple, flowing melodies, called plainchant, became part of the celebration of mass. The tradition survives to this day.

Plainchant, or plainsong, was originally passed on orally, varying in style from region to region or monastery to monastery. Then, to preserve traditions, religious communities began devising methods of writing down the music.

At first, signs were added to the text to give some indication of the rhythms. Later the signs were placed at different levels above the words to show where the melodies moved up or down in pitch.

In the 10th century, Guido d'Arrezzo (d 1050), an Italian monk and teacher, set down the idea of placing notes on or between a set of parallel lines – the stave – thus fixing their pitch in relation to each other.

Staff notation (writing music on a stave) is now established as the internationally recognised language of music, although, throughout history, many alternative systems have been developed and are used in different parts of the world.

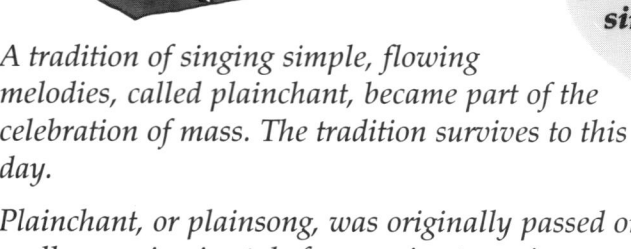

During this time, professional travelling musicians, minstrels, entertained people. From the 11th to the 13th centuries, groups of jugglers, dancers, acrobats and minstrels provided popular entertainment in town and countryside.

Popular dances and melodies were spread by the minstrels from country to country, and although many were not written down until later times, they survived in the folk dances and songs of the people.

Estampie royal
anon

The estampie is a 13th century dance performed to instrumental music. It was probably originated by the trouvères in the courts of France, but popularised outside court throughout Europe by the minstrels.

Eno sagrado en Vigo
• Aj ondas que eu vin veer
by Martin Codax

These two courtly love songs are by an early 13th century Spanish or Portuguese troubadour.

At the same time, male and female poet-musicians, based in royal courts, and often themselves courtiers of noble birth, were composing sophisticated songs for the entertainment of the nobility of Europe. They sang of chivalry, love, nature, and tales of the Crusades.

The poet-musician was called a troubadour in Southern Europe, and a trouvère in France.

Music of this time was based on different sets of notes from those most commonly used later. These sets of notes were known as modes. You can hear what they sound like by playing any set of eight adjacent white keys on a keyboard, eg D E F G A B C D.
The modes survive in some folk and jazz music.

5

Columba aspexit

What you need to know about the music

Composer: Hildegard of Bingen (1098–1179)

Hildegard was educated from the age of eight at a Benedictine nunnery. She became Abbess of the nunnery when she was 38, and later moved to the convent of Bingen (in modern Germany).

She wrote extensively on theology, natural history, medicine and the many visions she had seen since childhood. Through extensive letter-writing, she was involved in diplomacy and politics, spreading her fame across Europe.

Hildegard was also a musician, who composed many large-scale devotional songs, of which *Columba aspexit* is an example. The Latin text presents a vivid picture of Saint Maximinus celebrating mass, and was probably written for the abbey of which he was patron.

Features of the music

- The melody does not have a steady beat, but flows freely, following the rhythm of the words

- The melody moves mostly step-by-step to higher or lower notes, with few jumps in pitch

- There are many examples of melisma – one syllable of the text stretched over two or more notes of the melody, eg *bal-sa——— mum*

- One singer leads with the first line of text, then alternates with a group of voices singing together.

Drone accompaniment

The singers are accompanied by a symphony (see the instrument opposite) playing a drone. A drone – the repetition of a single note or combination of notes throughout a piece of music – was a common accompaniment to music of this time.

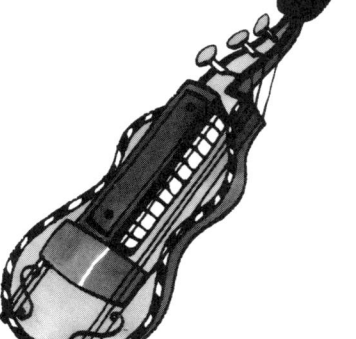

Symphony – hurdy gurdy

The symphony, or hurdy gurdy, was a popular instrument during the 12th century, used for both religious and secular music. It was the first instrument to combine strings with a keyboard.

The player turns a wheel which vibrates drone strings (see page 4). As well as this drone, a melody can be played on a keyboard which operates a separate string or strings. Hurdy gurdies are still used today in French and Belgian folk music.

Columba aspexit
(first four verses with translation)

Columba aspexit	*The dove peered in*
per cancellos fenestre,	*through the lattices of the window,*
ubi ante faciem eius,	*where, before its face,*
sudando sudavit balsamum	*a balm exuded*
de lucido Maximino.	*from incandescent Maximin.*
Calor solis exarsit	*The heat of the sun burned*
et in tenebras resplenduit:	*dazzling into the gloom:*
unde gemma surrexit	*whence a jewel sprang forth*
in edificantione templi	*in the building of the temple*
purissimi cordis benivoli.	*of the purest loving heart.*
Iste turris excelsa,	*He, the high tower,*
de ligno Libani et cipresso facta,	*constructed of Lebanon wood and cypress,*
iacincto at sardio ornata est,	*has been adorned with jacinth and diamonds,*
urbs precellens artes	*a city excelling the crafts*
aliorum artificum.	*of other builders.*
Ipse velox cervus cucurrit	*This swift hart sped*
ad fontem prissime aque	*to the fountain of clearest water*
fluentis de fortissimo lapide	*flowing from the most powerful stone*
qui dulcia aromata irrigavit.	*which courses with delightful spices.*

Activity 1   *Exploring notation*

Each child will find a way to notate a simple melody they have first composed using three next-door notes.

What you will need
– for each child a set of chime bars (or other tuned percussion) with three next-door notes, eg DEF or EFG.

Listen to track 1 Columba aspexit

After listening, tell the children that this music was composed nearly one thousand years ago, long before sound recording was invented.

Ask the children how they think the music was passed on from generation to generation. (It was written down.) Explain that musicians in monasteries were only just beginning to find ways of writing down music (see page 6).

What to do
• Each child needs to prepare a short descriptive piece of prose (30–50 words) to set to music. It may be about themselves or related to a class topic.

• Before they begin composing, explain that they will need to record the pitches of the melody notes in writing in order to remember them. Discuss their ideas for doing this, eg

• Next, the children individually use a set of chime bars to compose a melody for their words, notating it in their chosen way.

What to assess
Listen to the melodies together, discussing the different notations the children have devised.
What problems arose? (Letter names alone don't help the reader to see the shape of the melody. A line showing the shape doesn't say which note to sing, etc.)

Activity 2   *Writing a melody on line notation*

In pairs, the children will notate their melodies using a horizontal line to indicate the relationship of one note to another and to show the shape of the melody.

What you will need
– chime bars as before
– a worksheet (page 8) and a pencil each

Listen to track 1 Columba aspexit

Ask the children to draw the melody with one hand in the air as they listen. How does the melody move – step-by-step or jumping around? (Smoothly, step-by-step most of the time.)

Line with letter names of notes:

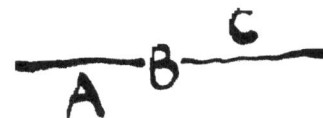

Line with symbols for notes:

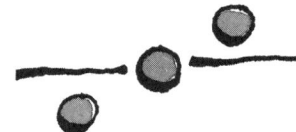

What to do
• Remind the children of the problems they found in writing down pitch.

• Explain that early musicians had the same problems. The idea they settled on (which eventually led to modern staff notation) was to use a horizontal line to show the relationship of higher to lower notes.

• Each child now writes down their own melody on the worksheet using either letter names or symbols.

• With their partner, they sing and play each melody in turn, reading from their notation.

Does the performance highlight more problems? Are there other things than pitch to show? (Some notes may be longer than others, more than one note may be sung to one syllable.) What additions or revisions might be made to assist an accurate performance?

What to assess
Have the children understood how notation needs to indicate pitch clearly, and that pitch alone is not enough – rhythm needs to be shown as well? (Notation went on developing until this was achieved.)

Writing a melody on line notation

Use letter names or symbols, and write them under, on, or above the line.
Write the words of your melody underneath on the dotted line.

Write the names of your notes here:

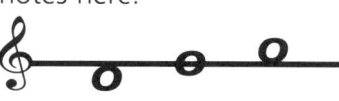

Photocopiable worksheet

Activity 3

Adding a drone

Pairs of children add a drone to their melodies.

What you will need
– chime bars as before plus another instrument (eg chime bar or keyboard) which can play the lowest of the three notes.

Listen to track 1 Columba aspexit

Questions you might ask
How many voices are singing at the beginning? (One, a soloist.)
Does this change? (Yes, more voices join in, singing the same melody.)
Can you hear any instruments? (Yes, an instrument is quietly playing the same note all the time – a drone. It sounds like bagpipes. It is a symphony.)

What to do
• Discuss ways of making a continuous sound on the drone instrument, eg by alternating two beaters quickly on tuned percussion, or using a long keyboard sound.

• One child sings/plays their melody; the other plays a drone.

What to assess
Is the drone continuous?
Are the children listening to each other sensitively, eg are they beginning and ending together? Are they matching each other's volume?

What to do next

• Working in larger groups, the children use the line notation to teach each other's songs.

• Each composer/conductor can choose a different way of performing their song, eg solo voice with drone; all sing; solo voice and instrumental melody without drone.

Activity 4

The candle (see opposite)

Performing a medieval-style melody from line notation. (You can hear how this might sound on **track 2**.)

The candle

Work in small groups to rehearse and present a performance of *The candle*.

What you will need
– one tuned instrument with notes DEFGA

– one drone instrument with note D, or D and A

– a drum, maraca, tambourine and cymbal with soft beater

What to do

1. Work out the melody of *The candle* on tuned percussion. Here is a key to the letter names of the notes.

Take it in turns to play each line on tuned percussion, singing it back immediately. Practise like this until you can all sing the whole song together.

What do you think the curved lines over some of the notes mean?

2. Add a drone, using:

 or

3. Decide what sounds you will add on each line using drum, then maraca, then tambourine, then cymbal. Work out a way of writing down what you are playing. Write it in the space below the words.

It looks like a vol-ca-no, blue, white and purple

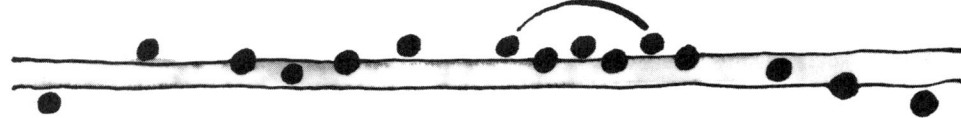

The wax is the la-va, craw——ling down the side

The flame is the la-va, ro-cket-ing in-to the sky

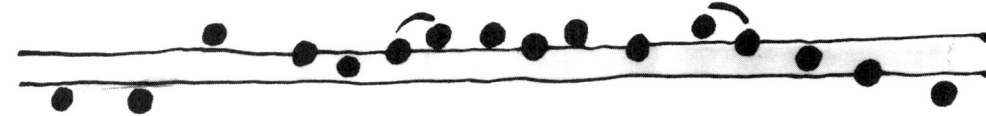

And the light is as bright as a mil-lion stars and the sun

Estampie royal

What you need to know about the music

Composer: anonymous (13th century)

Dance music and the estampie

Estampies are dances played on instruments. They were the first dances for pairs of men and women, each couple dancing together holding hands. Before the estampie, dances were performed with songs, everyone joining in with the dancing in a line or a circle.

Estampies were possibly the earliest form of purely instrumental music. They originated in Provence, then were spread through Europe by the troubadours (see page 5) who were escaping the Albigensian Crusades at the beginning of the 12th century.

Though the estampie was a very popular dance throughout Europe until the 14th century – often danced in the open air – only a few of its steps are known today.

The instruments

Many court musicians, who had travelled with the crusaders during the holy wars against the Muslims, heard instruments and music of North Africa and the Middle East, which influenced their own compositions.

This estampie is played on a traditional Moroccan hand-played frame drum with rattles (above left); and on medieval fiddle (below left; drawn from a contemporary illustration).

Features of the music

• A rousing rhythm is played on frame drum.

• The melody is played on the medieval fiddle.

• After a short drum introduction, the fiddle enters. There are two main sections, **A** and **B**, within which improvised (made up) melodies are alternated with a refrain (recurring melody). The piece ends with the drum played on its own again.

Activity 1

class

Understanding the structure

This activity helps the children understand the structure of *Estampie royal* by focussing their listening on the pattern of counts within the sections.

What you will need

– an enlarged plan of *Estampie royal* (opposite)

What to do and what to assess

• Teach yourself how to count along with the music using **track 3**, then see below. Assess the children's understanding of the number pattern through the questions and practical work below and opposite.

Listen to track 4 Estampie royal

• Pointing to the numbers one by one, count them out loud to the children as you listen together – count to eight twice for the introduction. Discuss the pattern the numbers fall into.

• Now divide the class into two groups to perform the piece like this, counting out loud along with the music in this order:

A sections		B sections	
Group 1	**Group 2**	**Group 1**	**Group 2**
❶ x 4	❷ x 7	❶ x 6	❷ x 7
❸ x 4	❹ x 8	❸ x 6	❹ x 8

• Repeat. Encourage the children to count silently after the introduction, while maintaining a steady clap/tap.

• Follow the plan as you listen to the music again. Count quietly. What do the children notice about the melody? *(The melody of the 7- and 8-count sections is the same – it starts on a low note, then jumps up. In the 4- and 6-count sections, the fiddle plays different music each time. It usually starts on higher notes.)*

Performing a percussion estampie

Work in two small groups to rehearse and present a percussion performance of *Estampie royal*.

What you will need
– an enlarged copy of the plan below
– two types of contrasting percussion sounds eg

drums for group 1   woodblocks for group 2

What to do
• Appoint a conductor to count the number pattern below while you play like this:

Group 1: play during the 4- and 6-count sections.
Group 2: play during the 7- and 8-count sections.

• Did you have any difficulties? What can you improve?

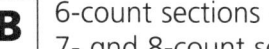

Improvising a percussion estampie

Work in small groups to make up a percussion piece.

What you will need
– an enlarged copy of the plan below
– untuned percussion instruments, eg drums, tambourines, bells.

What to do
Play it this way:

A   4-count sections – one plays (take turns to play)
7- and 8-count sections – everyone plays

B   6-count sections – one plays
7- and 8-count sections – everyone plays

• The person playing alone in the 4- and 6- count sections makes up (improvises) a rhythm.
• Everyone else decides on the same rhythm pattern to play during the 7- and 8- count sections.

	Counts
drum intro	1 2 3 4 5 6 7 8 1 2 3 4 5 6 7 8
A	1 2 3 4 1 2 3 4 5 6 7 1 2 3 4 1 2 3 4 5 6 7 8
A	1 2 3 4 1 2 3 4 5 6 7 1 2 3 4 1 2 3 4 5 6 7 8
B	1 2 3 4 5 6 1 2 3 4 5 6 7 1 2 3 4 5 6 1 2 3 4 5 6 7 8
A	1 2 3 4 1 2 3 4 5 6 7 1 2 3 4 1 2 3 4 5 6 7 8
B	1 2 3 4 5 6 1 2 3 4 5 6 7 1 2 3 4 5 6 1 2 3 4 5 6 7 8
B	1 2 3 4 5 6 1 2 3 4 5 6 7 1 2 3 4 5 6 1 2 3 4 5 6 7 8
B	1 2 3 4 5 6 1 2 3 4 5 6 7 1 2 3 4 5 6 1 2 3 4 5 6 7 8
ending	1 2 3 4 5 6 7 8

Eno sagrado en Vigo • Aj ondas que eu vin veer

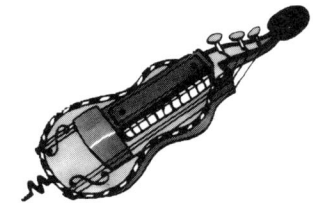

What you need to know about the music

Composer: Martin Codax (c1300)

Martin Codax was a highly successful troubadour in northern Spain at the beginning of the 14th century.

These two contrasting songs are from a set of seven poems and music, *Cantigas de amigo*, which were discovered in 1914 on a piece of parchment inside a book binding. They are in the voice of a woman from Vigo, who pines for her lover (amigo/amado) far away. The language is a local dialect.

Features of *Eno sagrado en vigo*

- The song has six short verses, each ending with a one line repeated refrain, 'amor ei'.
- The melody moves mostly step by step and uses a modal set of notes.
- A woman sings, accompanied by harp, symphony and a hand-played frame drum in this arrangement.
- The rhythms have a strong dance-like beat.
- At the end, the instruments drop out one by one, thinning the texture until only the drone (see page 6) is left. This leads into the next song.

Activity 1   Contrasts

Listen to track 5 Eno sagrado • Aj ondas

Compare the two pieces. As they listen, the children may like to move their hands and bodies. Ask how the two pieces make them feel. What differences did they notice between the two songs and any movements they made?

Listen again. What changes the mood? (Notice the tempo of the songs, the way the instruments accompany, the volume of the singing and playing.)

Read out the translations of the texts and compare these with the children's thoughts about the music. The first describes dancing in joy at being in love, the second calls to the sea in sadness at being separated from a loved one. Do the children agree that the music reflects the mood of the texts?

Features of *Aj ondas que eu vin veer*

- There are two short verses with very similar endings.
- The melody is slow and wistful, moving step by step and using a modal set of notes.
- A quiet drone on symphony drops out on the last line.
- The rhythm freely follows the words with much use of *melisma* – one syllable stretched across several notes.

Eno sagrado en Vigo

Eno sagrado en Vigo	*In Vigo and on holy ground,*
Beylava corpo velido.	*A body fair danced round and round,*
Amor ei.	*All in love am I.*
En vigo, no sagrado,	*In Vigo, in this holy place,*
Beylava corpo delgado.	*Danced so slim and full of grace,*
Amor ei.	*All in love am I.*
Beylava corpo delgado,	*Danced so slim and full of grace,*
Que nunc' ouver' amado.	*That ne'er had looked upon love's face,*
Amor ei.	*All in love am I.*
Beylava corpo velido,	*Danced a fair body round and round,*
Que nunc' ouver' amigo.	*That never had a lover found,*
Amor ei.	*All in love am I.*
Que nunc' ouver' amigo	*That never had a lover found,*
Ergas no sagrad', en Vigo.	*And danced there on holy ground,*
Amor ei.	*All in love am I.*
Que nunc' ouver' amado	*That never had looked upon love's face,*
Ergas en Vigo, no sagrado.	*And danced in this holy place,*
Amor ei.	*All in love am I.*

Aj ondas que eu vin veer

Aj ondas que eu vin veer,	*Waves that I came to see,*
Se me saberedes dizer	*Ah waves, say unto me*
Porque tarda meu amigo sen min?	*Why my love lingers away from me?*
Aj ondas que vin mirar,	*O waves that ebb and swell,*
Se me saberedes contar	*Will you not to me tell*
Porque tarda meu amado sen min?	*Why my love lingers thus away from me?*

Activity 2 — Composing to create a mood

The children work in small groups to set a medieval poem to a melody. The aim is to create a distinctive mood reflecting that of the words.

What you will need
– copies of either worksheet below for each group
– a cassette recorder
– a range of instruments, tuned and untuned

What to do
• Let the children work on their melodies and accompaniments using the worksheets below.

What to assess
How well does the melody express the mood of the words? Consider the use of tempo, rhythm, pitch and dynamics – have these been considered and used effectively?
Have any of the groups used a drone, or melisma?

Summer is a-coming in,
Loudly sing cuckoo.
Groweth seed and bloweth mead,
And spring the woods anew.
Sing cuckoo!

1. Work in a small group.

2. Read the poem out loud several times.

3. Discuss the words and mood of the poem.

4. Compose a melody for the words. Think about the rhythm and the speed of your melody. What would best match the mood of the words?

5. Record your song on cassette and listen to it. Can it be improved to match your words better?

6. Choose some instruments to play in an accompaniment.

7. Try out your ideas together. Does your accompaniment match the mood of the poem?

8. When you are ready, play your composition to the class.

9. You may like to write down the poem and music you have composed. Illustrate it as a medieval manuscript with pictures and colours, matching the mood of your music.

Photocopiable worksheet

Under the wood the sun now goes;
Mary, I'm sad for your cheek's
*   pale rose.*
Under the tree the Son goes too;
Mary, I'm sad for your son and you.

1. Work in a small group.

2. Read the poem out loud several times.

3. Discuss the words and mood of the poem.

4. Compose a melody for the words. Think about the rhythm and the speed of your melody. What would best match the mood of the words?

5. Record your song on cassette and listen to it. Can it be improved to match your words better?

6. Choose some instruments to play in an accompaniment.

7. Try out your ideas together. Does your accompaniment match the mood of the poem?

8. When you are ready play, your composition to the class.

9. You may like to write down the poem and music you have composed. Illustrate it as a medieval manuscript with pictures and colours, matching the mood of your music.

Photocopiable worksheet

Listening links

What you need to know about the music

O viridissima virga

Composer: Hildegard of Bingen (1098–1179)

The Latin text of this devotional song illustrates Hildegard's devotion to the Virgin Mary. The melody is sung first by a group of tenors (high male voices), then by a single tenor. The drone accompaniment (page 6) is played on the symphony (page 6).

Danse royale

Composer: anon French (c13th century)

A harp plays this court dance. The elegant, slow melody is for the type of graceful, walking dance which the lords and ladies would perform at banquets. (Staff notation is given on page 76.)

Onques n'amai tant que jou fui amee

Composer: Richart de Fournival (born in Amiens, c1201–60)

This lament –

   'I never loved as much as I was loved, now I repent – through my pride I have lost my love.'

is a 'chanson de femmes', intended to be performed by female court musicians. Its composer was a French poet-musician – trouvère. Twenty of his poems and six of his songs survive.

The song is accompanied by a medieval fiddle.

Track 6   O viridissima virga

1. [ ]

1. Name the instrument which plays the first sound in this music.

2. [ ]

2. What is the name for this kind of accompaniment?

3. [ ]

3. Are the voices high-sounding or low-sounding? Male or female?

4. [ ]

4. When do you hear a voice alone? When are there more voices?

5. [ ]

5. Where would this music have been performed?

6. [ ]

6. Who would have sung this song?

7. Design a medieval picture for the first letter of the song title.

7. [ ]

Track 7   *Danse royale*

1. What kind of instrument plays the melody?

> 1.

2. How do you think the sound is being made?

> 2.

3. Draw a picture of what you think the instrument looks like.

> 3.

4. Where would this piece have been performed? (Clue in the title.)

> 4.

5. This is dance music. Listen again. What do you think the dance steps were like?

> 5.

6. Here is the first part of the melody. Choose a tuned instrument to play it. You will need notes **D E F♯ G A**. (Staff notation on page 76.)

1	2	3	1	2	3	1	2	3	1	2	3	1	2	3	1	2	3
A		A	A		GF♯	G		G		G		B		B	B		AG

1	2	3	1	2	3	1	2	3	1	2	3	1	2	3	1	2	3
A			A			D		E	G		G	A	GF♯	G	G		

Track 8   *Onques n'amai tant que jou fui amee*

1. What is the instrument you hear?

2. How is the sound being made?

3. How many voices are singing?

4. What kind of musician might have composed this song?

5. Listen again. Draw or write what you think the singer may be singing about.

This was an age of 'rebirth' throughout Europe with discoveries and advances in medicine and science (Copernicus, Fallopius, Leonardo da Vinci), architecture and art (Botticelli, Breughel, Michaelangelo, Titian), literature (Caxton, Dante, Shakespeare), and exploration (Columbus, Drake, Magellan, Vasco da Gama).

In Italy, composers of religious music were exploiting the resonant acoustics of the great churches, including St Peter's in Rome and St Mark's in Venice.

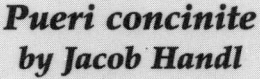

Pueri concinite
by Jacob Handl

Many European composers were inspired by musical developments in Italy, and adapted these developments to their own compositions. Handl's vocal music is said to have been influenced by the composers Andrea and Giovanni Gabrieli who made a huge impact on the musical and religious world with the scale and magnificence of their work at St Mark's in Venice during the second half of the 16th century.

Religious music was often very elaborate. Many voices sang overlapping melodies, creating a seamless blend of ethereal sounds, which almost rendered the words indistinguishable. This technique of writing many overlapping parts is called polyphony (many sounding). In contrast, the technique of antiphony (sounding against) produced a different texture by bouncing single words or phrases from one part of the choir to another. Both techniques of writing were wonderfully effective in resonant churches.

Music flourished outside the church too. Town and city corporations set up bands to play at civic functions, and in the countryside, villagers had their own songs and dances. The first printed music appeared in the second half of the 15th century.

Martin
said to his man

Published in 1609 by Thomas Ravenscroft, this four-part drinking song is sung in folk clubs to this day. Singers make up their own nonsense words to it.

By the time of Henry VIII in later Tudor times, visitors were often received in the comfort of the privy chamber and the musicians adapted to this more intimate arrangement accordingly. They tended to play in adjoining rooms with open doors and often scaled down the number of players as necessary. The gradual disuse of the halls for this type of smaller scale entertainment spread across Europe.

In England in early Tudor times, the hall was the setting for banquets and dancing in wealthy households with the musicians playing in the minstrels' gallery. Dancing was an important part of this upper class social life and many styles, emerging in different countries, became popular throughout Europe. The estampie (page 10) had set the pattern for partner dances, and now most dances were variations of the same basic steps.

During the Tudor period these 'court' dances had divided into two types – elegant, walking dances for the older guests, and lively, energetic dances for the younger.

Mistress Winter's jump by John Dowland

As its name suggests, this is a lively court dance, and probably one of the kind which allowed pairs of dancers to show off their skills by improvising complex steps, known as 'tricks', while others gathered around to watch.

There was a great increase in the composition and publication of instrumental music, particularly for the middle classes to play in their own homes.

Instruments were often played together in families of the same type, known as consorts. For example, many homes would have a chest of viols (string instruments which predate the modern string family stored in a chest), or recorders, which they would play, sitting around a table, from specially printed music which allowed all players to read the music at once.

Pueri concinite

What you need to know about the music

Composer: Jacob Handl (1550–1591)

Handl was a Cistercian monk who travelled the monasteries of Eastern Europe as a composer and choirmaster in order to develop his music.

Features of the music

Pueri concinite is for four unaccompanied male voices: two trebles (high), one alto (upper middle), one tenor (lower middle). The Latin text celebrates the birth of Christ. Handl incorporates a lilting 15th century German carol melody (*Joseph dearest, Joseph mine*) on the words 'quod divina voluit clementia.'

Handl skilfully uses contrasting textures (ways of combining sounds) in this short piece to provide colour and interest, and to reinforce the meaning of the words. The textures (**track 9** helps you to recognise them in *Pueri concinite*) have been given simpler names for the purposes of the activities:

- **homophony** (blocks) – voices singing the same words together, used here to emphasise celebrating in unity
- **antiphony** (ping pong) – different voices bounce words back and forth, used here to show excitement.
- **polyphony** (relays) – separately-moving, overlapping voices, used here to give a joyful impression of many voices raised in individual praise.

Pueri concinite

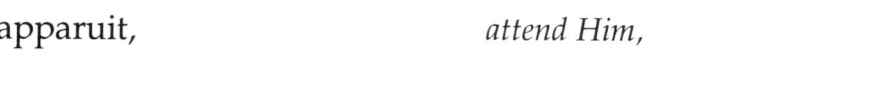

Pueri concinite, nato regi psallite,	*Sing praises to the child, God our King,*		**Relays – polyphony** The voices start one after the other, and continue to overlap each other in waves of running melodies.
pia voce dicite (x 3)	*with sweet voices*		**Blocks – homophony** The voices sing these words together to show unity.
apparuit,	*attend Him,*		**Ping pong – antiphony** The word bounces back and forth between the voices giving an exciting lift to the sound.
quem genuit Maria.	*born of the Virgin Mary.*		**Blocks** as above.
Sunt umpleta quae praedixit Gabriel:	*These things which Gabriel foretold have been fulfilled:*		**Relays** The voices overlap again as they each sing the lilting, rising and falling melody.
eia	*behold*		**Ping pong** as above.
virgo Deum genuit, quod divina voluit clementia.	*the Virgin begat our Lord Who came down lovingly in His divine mercy.*		**Blocks** The last words of the text are repeated and the voices sing together.

Activity 1 *Blocks, relays and ping pong*

Class

The children will perform a simple melody using a variety of textures (you can hear all these on **track 10**). The melody is from the German carol which Handl used.

1	2	3	4	5	6	1	2	3	4	5	6	1	2	3	4	5	6
F		G	A		B♭	C'		B♭	A		G	F		G	A		
Sing	a	song	to	ce	-	le -	brate	at	Christ - mas-time								

What to do
• Texture 1 – Blocks
Teach all the children the melody above (staff notation on page 76).

• All sing the words together three or four times without a break.

• Texture 2 – Relays
Now divide the class into three groups and sing the melody with one group starting after another, overlapping each other –

• Texture 3 – Ping pong
Ask the children (still in three groups) to suggest single words they can sing, bouncing each from one group to another. The children will need to decide on some notes to sing, a rhythm and an order, eg (**track 10**):

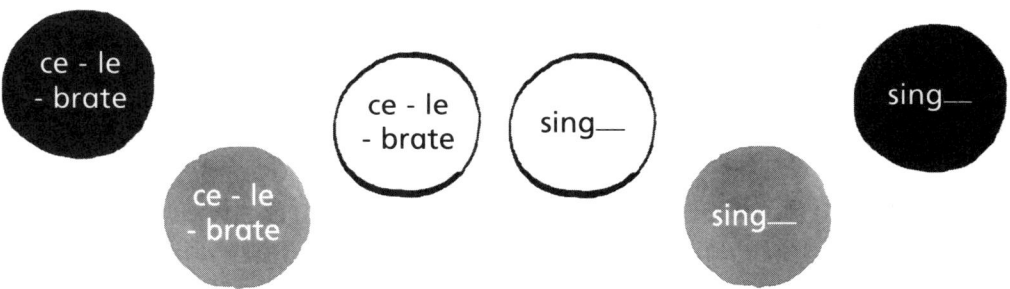

Class performance
Now decide in which order to use these three textures in a whole class piece for voices, eg

What to assess
Use the listening box below to assess the children's understanding of the textures they have used.

Listen to track 11 Pueri concinite
Read the Latin text and its translation to the children.

Questions you might ask
Can you identify any similarities between this music and ours? (The textures are those we used in our piece. We heard our melody in it.)

Listen again as many times as necessary. Discuss the textures with the children asking them to say which they recognise and in which order they hear them (the chart on page 18 shows you the answers to this).

Activity 2

 *Class*

Instrumental textures

Now the children will use the same three textures as the basis for a class instrumental piece.

What you will need

– a selection of tuned and untuned instruments – one per child. Tuned notes – F G A B♭C'
– one or more copies of each worksheet per group

What to do and what to assess

• Divide the class into three groups, corresponding to the three textures:

group 1 **group 2** **group 3**

• The children may choose whether to play only the rhythm of the words, or to play the melodies as well. Each group will devise a section of music using the appropriate texture.

• When the groups have completed their sections, listen to each separately. Are there any problems to solve, eg are the separate relay parts clear?

• Finally discuss and decide in which order to play the three sections to make a whole class piece. Ask the children to suggest different orders. Listen to and then discuss their preferences. (Note: the individual group pieces will not necessarily be performed at the same speed – do the children think this should affect their decisions?)

Draw a plan of the final class piece (individual children may draw plans of their favourite order as well) eg

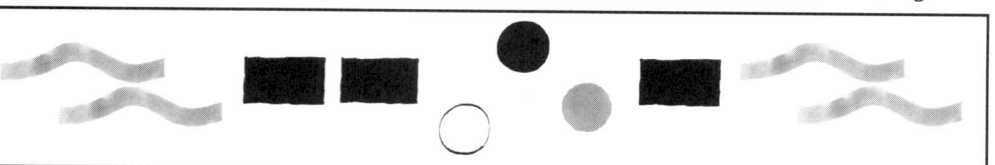

Group 1

Blocks

You are going to arrange one section of a class piece of music.

What you will need

– one instrument each, untuned or tuned with notes F G A B♭ C'

What to do

1. Clap this rhythm pattern together, saying the words out loud then in your heads. Count a steady 1 2 3 4 5 6 before you begin.

1	2	3	4	5	6	1	2	3	4	5	6	1	2	3	4	5	6
Sing		a	song		to	ce -		le - brate		at Christ -		mas	time				

Were you clapping together at the same speed? Try to improve your teamwork. Can you repeat the pattern several times and still keep together?

2. Work out how to play the pattern on your instrument. Untuned – play the rhythm you clapped. Tuned – play these notes.

1	2	3	4	5	6	1	2	3	4	5	6	1	2	3	4	5	6
F		G	A		B♭	C'		B♭	A		G	F		G	A		

3. Now practise playing all together. Remember to keep a steady beat. Practise at a slow speed first, until you can all play tidily together, then speed up a little.

4. Now you are ready to plan your section of the class piece. Decide how many times you will play the pattern and what speed you will play at.

Photocopiable worksheet

Group 2   *Relays*

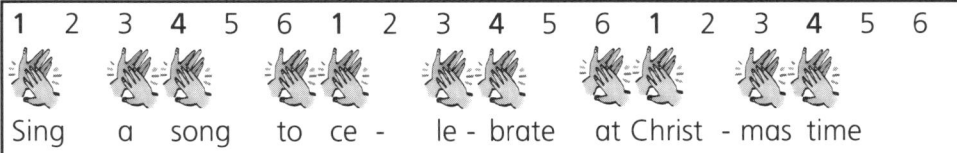

You are going to arrange one section of a class piece of music.

What you will need
– one instrument each, untuned or tuned with notes F G A B♭ C'

What to do
1. Clap this rhythm pattern together, saying the words out loud then in your heads. Count a steady **1** 2 3 **4** 5 6 before you begin.

1	2	3	4	5	6	1	2	3	4	5	6	1	2	3	4	5	6
Sing		a	song		to	ce –		le -	brate		at	Christ -		mas	time		

Were you clapping together at the same speed? Try to improve your teamwork.

2. Now clap in relays, starting one after another:

3. Work out how to play the pattern on your instrument then play in relays. Untuned – play the rhythm you clapped. Tuned – play these notes.

1	2	3	4	5	6	1	2	3	4	5	6	1	2	3	4	5	6
F		G	A		B♭	C'		B♭	A		G	F		G	A		

4. Now you are ready to plan your section of the class piece. Decide on the speed, the number of times you will play the pattern, and the order to play in.

Group 3   *Ping pong*

You are going to arrange one section of a class piece of music.

What you will need
– one instrument each, untuned or tuned with notes F G A B♭ C'

What to do
1. Choose three or four separate words.

2. Work out a simple rhythm and melody for each word within a count of six beats, eg

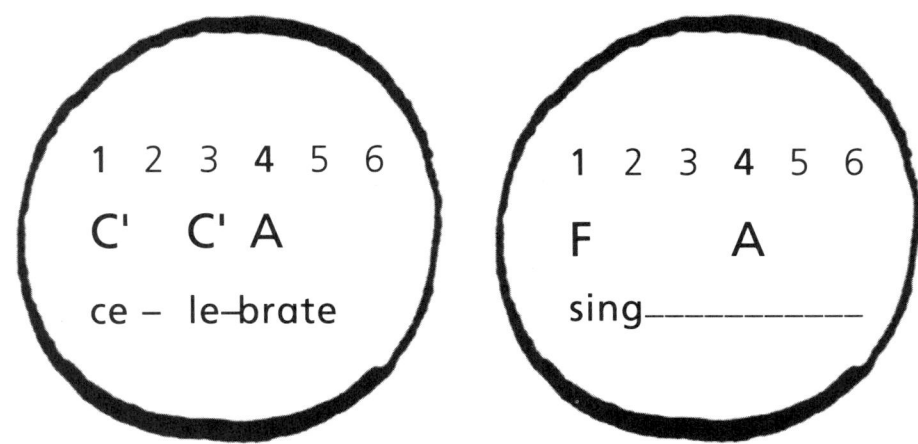

When you have tried out your patterns write them down.

3. Practise playing the patterns on your instruments, then divide into groups to pass them back and forth. Decide how you will do this. How quickly or slowly will you play? Which order will the groups play in? Will each group play the patterns louder or quieter or just the same? Do you want to change the combination of instruments in any of the groups?

4. When you have planned this, you will be ready to play your section of the class piece.

Martin said to his man

What you need to know about the music

Composer: Thomas Ravenscroft (1590–c1635)

This song was published by Ravenscroft in 1609 in a collection of three- and four-part songs and rounds, *Deuteromelia*. Most of the songs are settings of humorous and popular poems including the first known printing of *Three blind mice*.

Although Ravenscroft was a learned church musician and music theorist, he was determined to write music for all tastes: for 'court, city and country'.

Features of the music

This tavern song describes the impossible visions of one who has 'well drunken'. It is composed for four voices: soprano (high), alto (upper middle), tenor (lower middle) and bass (low). After the first verse and chorus each singer has a chance to make up new words, while the others sing the repeated chorus lines.

Activity 1   Singing Martin said to his man

Class

The children learn the song thoroughly.

What you will need
– copies of the song sheet opposite
– **track 12** (first verse) (staff notation on page 76)

What to do and what to assess
• Use the recording on track 12 to teach the song.
• Let the children hear the melody several times, then ask them to join in on the chorus lines. When these are secure, sing the whole melody.
• Now sing without the recording, learning the other verses. Give the children a clear direction of when to start, and at what speed, eg count 1 – 2 – to begin.
• Assess how confidently and clearly they can sing the song together from memory, then encourage individuals to sing alone as in the recording (**track 13**).

Activity 2   Adding new words

Pairs of children make up new words to the song.

What to do
• Ask each pair to make up a new verse from two nonsensical happenings. The ends of the two new lines will need to rhyme (see lines 5–6 opposite), eg

... I saw an ant eat a whale and a supersonic snail ...

... I saw a web spin a spider and an apple drinking cider...

... I saw a chicken chase a fox and a Jack jump in a box ...

What to assess
• When each pair has devised new words which fit smoothly into the song, and which rhyme, sit the class in a circle. Sing the song again with the new verses. Each pair will sing their own verse, either together or one line each, with everyone joining in with the chorus.

Listen to track 13 Martin said to his man

Questions you might ask
What are the similarities and differences between this song and our version? (It is the same song; neither uses instruments; the singers take turns to sing alone; in this music the voices sing different parts, while we all sing the same melody together.)

Martin said to his man

Martin said to his man,
  Fie, man, fie!
Martin said to his man,
  Who's the fool now?
Martin said to his man,
'Fill thou the cup and I the can.'
  Thou hast well drunken, man,
  Who's the fool now?
  Thou hast well drunken, man,
  Who's the fool now?

I saw a goose ring a hog,
  Fie, man, fie!
I saw a goose ring a hog,
  Who's the fool now?
I saw a goose ring a hog,
And the snail bite a dog ...

I saw a mouse catch a cat,
  Fie, man, fie!
I saw a mouse catch a cat,
  Who's the fool now?
I saw a mouse catch a cat,
And the cheese eat a rat ...

I saw a maid milk a bull,
  Fie, man, fie!
I saw a maid milk a bull,
  Who's the fool now?
I saw a maid milk a bull,
Every pull a bucketfull ...

Write and illustrate your own verses here:

fie = an exclamation of disgust or disapproval

Photocopiable songsheet

Mistress Winter's jump

What you need to know about the music

Composer: John Dowland (1563–1626)

Dowland wished to be appointed as a court musician to Elizabeth I in 1594. He was unsuccessful, probably because he was a Catholic during a time when royalty favoured Protestantism. He was a highly-skilled lute player and singer and was famed for his performances throughout Europe. Many of his compositions survive in manuscript and a few were printed. They show him to be one of the most gifted composers of the period. He wrote collections of songs and many pieces for lute. In 1612 he achieved his ambition and became lutenist to the court of James I.

Features of the music

• This energetic dance is based on a pattern of eight counts. The dance melody is in two repeated sections (staff notation on page 77):

Section 1	Repeat	Section 2	Repeat
A	A	B^1 B^2	B^1 B^2
1–8	9–16	17–32	33–48

• The dance is played twice on this recording:

1st time: violin plays the melody, accompanied by bass viol, guitar, lute and mandora (a small high-pitched lute often played with a plectrum). Listen out for the decorations (improvised embellishments) played on the mandora.

2nd time: the violin repeats the melody; the mandora has an even more decorative part.

• The piece begins and ends with a reverence – one long-sounding chord played while the dancers bow.

Activity 1   Performing Mistress Winter's jump

Instructions for a dance based on authentic steps of the period are on the page opposite. It gives an idea of the stepping and jumping dance which may have been performed by Mistress Winter herself.

Many popular dances of the time were based on two steps: the simple and the double, performed either stepping forwards or backwards. This diagram shows you the steps moving forward (count to four):

1 left step **2** close **3** right step **4** close
simple forward

1 left step **2** right step **3** left step **4** close
double forward

Pairs of dancers would begin by facing the host and hostess, or if they themselves were dancing, the place in the hall where they sat. The B1 parts of the dance give the opportunity for each couple to make up steps or 'tricks' as in the Elizabethan fashion of improvising fancy, athletic steps as additions to the basic dance.

What to do and what to assess

• Teach one section at a time without the music. (You can hear the dance steps called on **track 14**). Encourage the children to look ahead, taking small, neat steps no more than a foot's length for good balance and elegance.

• Arrange the pairs in a block facing forward. All the pairs will move forward slightly during B2.

• Perform the dance to **track 15**. Can the children remember the steps accurately, show good balance, and move neatly but not stiffly in time to the music?

RENAISSANCE

Mistress Winter's jump

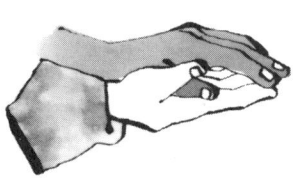

Read the steps from bottom to top. The order of sections and of simple forward, back, tricks etc reads from left to right. Sample steps for B1 and its repeat are given, but the idea is to make up your own.

Each pair hold hands – boy's right palm upwards with thumb curled over girl's left palm resting on top.

Reverence – at beginning and end

Girl bends knees slightly and rises slowly.

Boy removes 'hat' and sweeps left arm down to side while stepping back on right foot and bending right knee. Left leg stretched in front.

Both look ahead.

	A	A	B¹	B²	B¹	B²
8	close	**R**	girl jumps up	close	**R**	**R**
7	right step back	**E**	girl hops left	right step back	**E**	**E**
6	close	**P**	boy jumps up	close	**P**	**P**
5	left step back	**E**	girl jumps up	left step back	**E**	**E**
4	close	**A**	boy jumps up	close	**A**	**A**
3	right step forward	**T**	boy hops left	left step forward	**T**	**T**
2	close		girl jumps up	right step forward		
1	left step forward		boy jumps up	left step forward		

simple forward (1–4), simple back (5–8), repeat   **make up tricks (1–8)**   **double forward (1–4), double back (5–8)**   **repeat**

Listening links

What you need to know about the music

Packington's pound

Composer: anon (16th century)

Packington's pound was one of the most popular Elizabethan tunes. It was reused again and again in songs and instrumental pieces. This version is arranged for the outdoors, perhaps to play on a street corner or in a slow procession. The loud shawm, which plays the melody, and the drum would have quickly summoned up a crowd to gather round and listen.

The piece is in three sections. The first (played twice) and last have almost the same rhythm but the melody is altered. The middle section is different in rhythm and melody.

In nomine

Composer: Richard Alwood (mid 16th century)

This piece is for chamber organ – a small, portable instrument, often used for secular music during the renaissance. It would have been played to the patron and guests as they ate in their private apartments. Alwood, like many composers of his time, uses a pre-existing melody, in this case a plainchant (see page 4), as the basis around which to weave new melodies. The slow plainchant is hardly noticeable. A new, fast, three-note rising melody overlaps many times in higher and lower-sounding parts of the keyboard.

Suzanna

Composer: John Dowland (1563–1626)

This lilting, three-beat piece for dancing or listening to is played by a consort (page 19) of lutes – two lutes and a theorbo (a bass lute). In performance, Dowland and his contemporaries often improvised skilfully on simple melodies. This piece gives an idea of the way they added decorations.

Track 16   Packington's pound

Follow the rhythm of this piece as you listen several times.

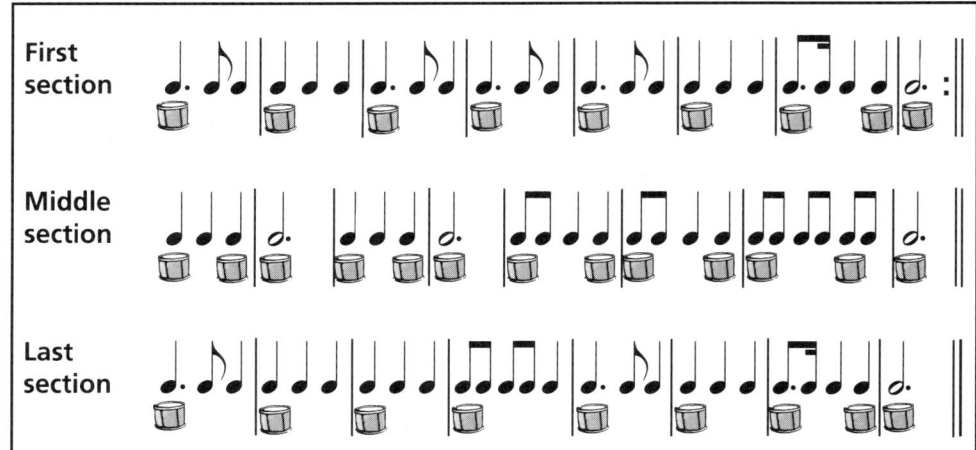

1. Listen carefully to the first and last sections – careful! the first section is repeated. These sections have a very similar rhythm, but it is not exactly the same. With a pencil, draw a circle round the part of the rhythm in the last section which is different from the rhythm in the first section.

2. Listen carefully to the drum rhythm. Where is the rhythm the same? Where is it different?

2.

3. Would this music be played inside or outdoors. How do you know?

3.

4.

4. In a small group play the rhythms on percussion instruments. One person plays the steady drum rhythm. Choose instruments which would be suitable for a procession around the playground. Write your choices here.

Photocopiable worksheet

Track 17   In nomine

Tudor kings and queens, such as Queen Elizabeth I, listened to music like this as they ate with guests at the royal palaces. It was played by court musicians.

1. What is the instrument you hear called?

1.

2. Where are you most likely to hear one today?

2.

3. Use a reference book or CDRom to find out how the sound of the instrument is made. Draw a diagram or describe in your own words what you discover.

3.

4. Play this melody on a recorder or xylophone:

4.	count	**1**	**2**	**3**	**4**
	play	**D E F**		**E**	**D**

5.

5. Listen to the piece several times. Listen closely to the way the first three notes of the melody you played appear over and over again. Are they always the same, or do you hear them played lower and higher as well?

Track 18   Suzanna

1. This piece is played on three lutes. How is the sound made on a lute?

1.

2. What did the Elizabethans call a group of instruments of the same type?

2.

3. Tap your fingers or conduct as you listen. How are the beats grouped in this piece?

3.

4. Do some research to find out more about lutes and lute music. Read about other Tudor musicians who composed for the lute. Draw a picture of a lute or lute player and write about what you have discovered here.

4.

Baroque
c1600–c1750

The term 'baroque' comes from the Portuguese word 'barocco' meaning encrusted, or rough, pearl. It was originally used in a derogatory way by critics of the elaborately decorated music of the time. Both architecture and music became more dramatic and ornate.

A great expansion of instrumental music and new musical structures took place during this time.

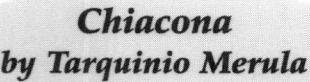

Chiacona
by Tarquinio Merula

The chaconne (French spelling) was originally a dance, which became a popular structure for instrumental music. A chaconne contains a ground bass – a repeating pattern of notes played by the lowest-sounding instrument in a group. The ground bass provides a simple foundation over which the other players can perform elaborate decorations.

Two modes (page 5) were being used more and more and came to be known as the major and minor keys, while the other modes fell into disuse. The pattern of notes in a major or minor scale is always the same, whatever the starting note – a major scale starting on C (C D E F G A B C) sounds the same – but a little higher in pitch – if the starting note is D (D E F# G A B C# D). Composers could now move from one key to another within one piece of music. Baroque composers explored and established all the major and minor keys and the colourful relationships between them.

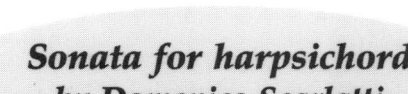

Sonata for harpsichord
by Domenico Scarlatti

Scarlatti is most famous for his 555 harpsichord sonatas. The term sonata (sound piece) had earlier been loosely applied to any instrumental music, large scale or small. Now it described a piece for a solo instrument or a small group. Scarlatti possessed an extraordinary inventiveness. Though he changed the overall structure of his sonatas very little, each was in detail unique.

The harpsichord was developed during the 15th century. Its strings are plucked by tiny splinters of quill in a mechanism operated from the keyboard. It remained a popular household instrument until the end of the 18th century – a four hundred year period, and throughout the baroque it played a key role in ensemble music of all kinds, and its repertoire of solo music was greatly expanded.

The baroque orchestra consisted mainly of string instruments of the violin family (violin, viola, cello and bass), which had replaced the viols in popularity. Sometimes a small number of woodwind or brass instruments were added.

A feature that was always present was the continuo part. This was performed by a small section of the orchestra playing the bass line of the music. A keyboard instrument such as organ or harpsichord was used to fill out the harmonies above the bass line. The keyboard player read from 'figured bass' - a number notation added to the written bass line. This suggested the chords to be played but allowed for personal interpretation by the performer, who was expected to improvise skilfully and appropriately.

The continuo section gave a very strong lead to the other musicians and the keyboard player, rather than a conductor, often directed the whole orchestra.

'Concerto' in renaissance times had literally meant instruments playing together (from the Italian word 'to get together'). During the baroque exciting developments took place, first producing the concerto grosso. In this type of concerto, the sound of a small group of instruments was contrasted with that of a large group, producing vivid effects. This led by the end of the 17th century to the solo concerto, in which the sound of one instrument played by a virtuoso was contrasted with that of the whole orchestra. Most of these concertos were in three movements (separate sections) with contrasting speeds: fast slow fast.

Vocal music, both secular and religious, also flourished. Following the Reformation, religious music was no longer restricted to Latin texts. Composers used their local languages to aid the congregation's understanding of the service. One of the many forms used was the cantata (sung piece), a collection of solos, duets and choruses for voices and chamber orchestra.

Second movement from Recorder concerto
by Antonio Vivaldi

Vivaldi composed over 360 concertos for solo instrument and orchestra. Most were for his own instrument, the violin, but others were for recorder, oboe, bassoon, cello and mandolin. This movement (separate section) is the second of three marked: Allegro (fast) Adagio (slow) Allegro (fast).

Chiacona

What you need to know about the music

Composer: Tarquinio Merula (1595–1665)

Little is known of Merula's life, except for the information given on the title pages of his surviving compositions. He was an Italian church organist and court composer, and published several collections of church and secular music.

Features of the music

This chaconne (the French term is commonly used) comprises an impressive series of florid decorations over a simple repeating bass pattern – a ground bass. Players were expected to be able to improvise freely on the music written by the composer, and this chaconne shows off the virtuosity of the two cornett players who play the decorations. The ground bass is played by the very low-sounding bass sackbut. A harpsichord continuo accompaniment holds the whole effect together.

- The ground bass is heard alone first.
- The cornetts then play a simple melody over it.
- Next the two cornett players perform a series of very rapid and ornate embellishments – decorations – over the ground bass. They feature:

fast rising and falling runs of notes

downward leaps

fast shakes on pairs of next door notes

E F E

G
E   F
        E
    F   E
    D
        C

parallel movements

Cornett

This is a wind instrument made of leather-covered wood with finger holes similar to those of a recorder, but with a small cup-shaped mouthpiece like that of a brass instrument. It was used for all kinds of outdoor and indoor music throughout this period.

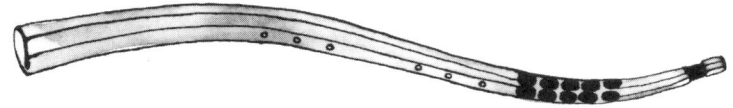

Sackbut

The forerunner of the modern trombone, a sackbut has a slide mechanism to alter the length of its metal tubing, and thus alter the pitch of the sounds it can produce. Sackbuts of different sizes were often played together in groups and were combined with cornetts in church and royal bands.

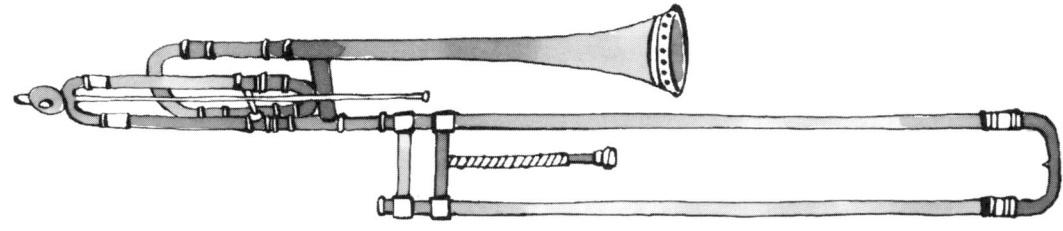

Activity 1

class

Decorating the ground bass

The children will learn to play the rhythm pattern of the ground bass (opposite), then individually will add body percussion decorations to it. The aim is to develop the skill of making two patterns fit together.

What to do and what to assess

- Teach the ground bass rhythm pattern (**track 19**). Can the children keep repeating this steadily?
- Next, in a circle, the whole class quietly claps the rhythm pattern, counting 1–12 in their heads (take care not to let the clapping get gradually faster).
- In turns, each child now adds body percussion decorations. Each improvises a new rhythm, starting on count 1 and ending on count 12 (example opposite on **track 20**). Do their new patterns fit in smoothly?

Ground bass rhythm pattern

count	10	11	12	1	2	3	4	5	6	7	8	9	10	11	12	repeat the boxed section
class claps				👏	👏		👏	👏		👏	👏		👏	👏		

Body percussion decorations (example)

count	10	11	12	1	2	3	4	5	6	7	8	9	10	11	12	1	2	3
class claps				👏	👏		👏	👏		👏	👏		👏	👏				

child 1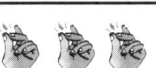

child 2

Activity 2

Chaconne for two players

Working in pairs, the children will devise an improvisation based on Merula's *Chiacona*. They will play Merula's melody and ground bass then add decorations – scales, shakes, parallels and two-note leaps – in the most effective ways they can find (for your reference and the children's if necessary, all these can be heard on **track 21**). After listening to Merula's music they will reconsider their own improvisations.

What you will need

– a copy of the worksheet, page 32 for each pair
– a tuned instrument with these notes:
G, A, B, C D E F G A B C' (staff notation on page 77)

What to do

• Let the children work on their improvisations using the worksheet on page 32.

• Listen to some of the improvisations, then listen to **track 22** *Chiacona*, focussing on the decorations – the fast scales, the shakes, leaps and parallels.

• After considering Merula's decorations, the children may wish to revise their own music, adding to or changing parts of it.

What to assess

Are the children able to keep the ground bass going steadily? Have the children chosen and ordered their decorations with care and deliberation? Are they able to say which decorations they feel work best?

Chaconne for two players

What you will need
– a tuned instrument each, or to share, with these notes

What to do

1. Each learn how to play the ground bass on your instrument. Can you play it over and over again without stopping? Keep counting quietly from 1 to 12.

2. Each learn how to play the melody on your instrument. Are you keeping a steady beat as you play? Keep counting quietly out loud or in your head.

3. Now one of you plays the ground bass while the other plays the melody. Count 10 11 12 so that you start on time:

| melody | 10 | 11 | 12 | 1 | E | E | E | D | C | etc |
| bass | 10 | 11 | 12 | C | C' | | C' | G | A | etc |

4. Decorations: melody player – now make up shakes, scales, leaps and parallels in any way you like. Try out different sequences and combinations of notes. Practise your ideas first on your own, then with your partner playing the ground bass. Do you want to change anything? Now swap parts.

5. Listen to *track 22 Chiacona* with your teacher, then if you like, make more changes to your improvisation. Decide on two final versions of your music then play them to the class.

Ground bass

Melody

Decorations

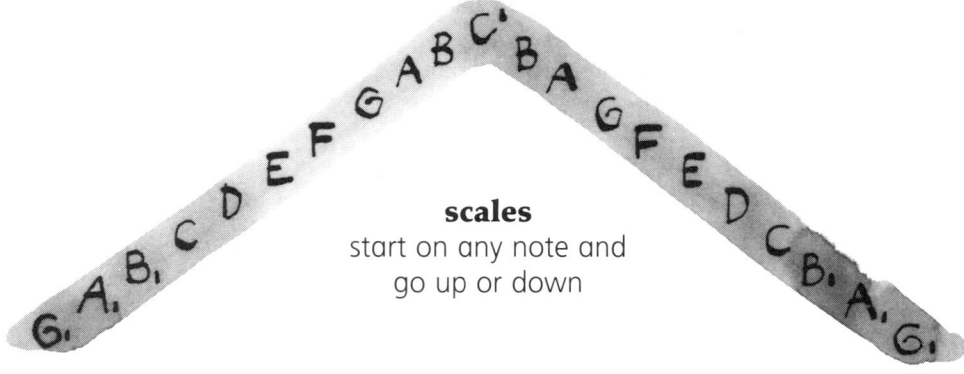

scales
start on any note and go up or down

leaps
jump down from one note to another

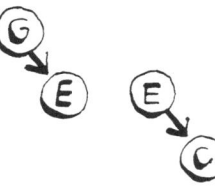

parallels
play any two notes together, then move to another two, then another two – keep moving

shakes
play any two next door notes very quickly

Listen to track 22 Chiacona

Use this plan to follow the music. It is not complete, but it will help you to help the children pick out the main features: ground bass, melody, and decorations.

The bass sackbut plays the ground bass twice with the harpsichord playing a continuo accompaniment (see page 29):

count	1	2	3	4	5	6	7	8	9	10	11	12	1	2	3	4	etc
ground bass	C	C'		C'	G		A	E		F	G		C	C'		C'	etc

One cornett plays a short melody, copied by the second cornett

count	1	2	3	4	5	6	7	8	9	10	11	12	1	2	3	4	etc
melody	E	E	E	D		C	G			F	E	D		C	E	E	E	etc

1st cornett   *2nd cornett*

Both cornetts add decorations over the ground bass including:

scales	**leaps**	**shakes**	**parallels**
fast, rising and falling scales played by both cornetts in turn	falling two-note leaps	next-door notes played quickly – first by one instrument then by two	parallel-moving pairs of notes
	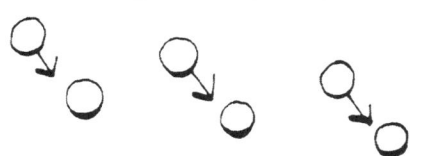	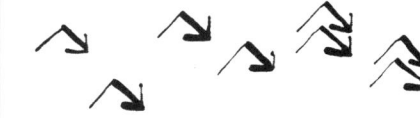	

The sackbut stops playing the ground bass and plays a new melody. It then resumes the ground bass and the cornetts add more decorations:

parallel-moving shakes	**slow three-note falling steps and turning shapes: singly then together**

Finally the ground bass is played very slowly with rising scales played by the cornetts.

Questions you might ask
How is this piece similar to yours? (We played the same ground bass and melody; we used the same type of decorations.)
Which of the decorations you used can you recognise in this music?
How does the composer use the two cornetts? (They take turns; play

together; copy one another. Their decorations are very fast and exciting.)

Listen again, noticing the bass sackbut all the way through.
Does the bass sackbut play the ground bass all the time? (No, in the middle of the piece it stops and plays a long melody which moves up and down.)

Sonata for harpsichord

What you need to know about the music

Composer: Domenico Scarlatti (1685–1757)

Scarlatti belonged to a very musical, Italian family. He first learned to play the organ and harpsichord with his father, Alessandro, who was a successful composer and music teacher. He became a friend of Handel, when they met in Venice in 1708, and in a contest to discover which of the two was the better keyboard player, the general opinion was that Handel slightly excelled as an organist, but as a harpsichordist, Scarlatti was his equal.

In 1729, Scarlatti was appointed to the Spanish court where he composed, towards the end of his life, an incredible 555 sonatas for harpsichord (see page 28).

Features of the music

• Most of his sonatas have only a single, unbroken movement containing two contrasting sections (binary structure **A B**). This one, unusually has a third section very similar to the first (ternary structure, **A B A**).
• Listen out for the higher and lower parts played by the right and left hands respectively – they play almost equal roles in the musical interest.

A is in the major key (giving a bright, cheerful mood):
• lively falling then rising patterns played by both hands moving in parallel; trills (quickly alternated adjacent notes) are added for decoration;
• falling sequences of skipping rhythms in the lower part;
• downward leaps in the lower part and wide upward leaps in the upper part;
• the lower part skipping rhythm is combined with the upper part moving two notes apart in parallel.

B is in the minor key (giving a more sombre mood):
• short, falling melodies are repeated;
• an exciting build up of notes played together leads to
• a very fast falling run of notes – a scale.

A returns in the major key with some small changes.

Activity 1   Dominoes

Pairs or small groups of children will investigate binary structure (**A B**), composing short pieces of music focussing on the musical elements. Later they will extend their pieces into ternary structure (**A B A**).

What you will need
– a copy of the worksheet for each pair or group
– a variety of instruments with different sounds

What to do
• Stage 1: each group will choose one domino and compose a short piece of music.

• Stage 2: the children develop these pieces by using two dominoes simultaneously.

• Stage 3: now they will change binary form into ternary form – ABA. The final A section does not have to be identical to the first but should be very similar.

• Stage 4: they will compose more ternary pieces exploring further contrasts, eg black keys/white keys/black keys, pluck/blow/pluck, etc.

What to assess
Listen to the results at each stage. The A and B sections should be different and should clearly represent the chosen element, eg a loud/quiet domino should have a clear difference in volume between the A and B sections. Can the rest of the class identify each group's domino and the elements used?

Listen to track 23 Sonata for harpsichord

Questions you might ask
What are your first impressions of this piece?
Did you notice how the piece is organised? (It has three sections, the first section returns at the end. It is in ternary form, A B A.)

Dominoes

Work in pairs or small groups.

Stage 1 – binary structure, AB

Bi means two. (Think of bicycle – two wheels, biped – two legs, binoculars – for two eyes.) Binary music has two sections of music which are different from each other. They can be labelled **A** and **B**.

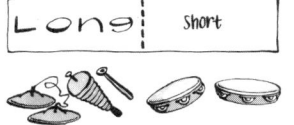

1. Choose one domino card.

2. Make up a short piece of music with two sections, A and B, using the two contrasts on the card. You can swap the order if you prefer. Think carefully about the instruments you will choose – the aim is to make what is on your domino clear to the listeners.

Stage 2

1. You can combine another domino with your first domino to make a more complicated piece of music. Choose a second domino and think how you can adapt your A and B sections to include the contrasts.

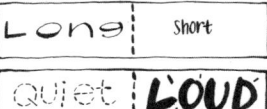

Stage 3 – ternary structure, ABA

1. Ternary means three sections of music. The last is very similar to the first. Make your piece into ternary form, **A B A**.

2. When you have tried out your ideas, record and listen to your ternary piece. Will the listeners recognise the A section when it returns?

Stage 4

1. Can you think of another type of contrast which you might use to make a new piece in ternary form?

2. When you are happy with your idea write it here:

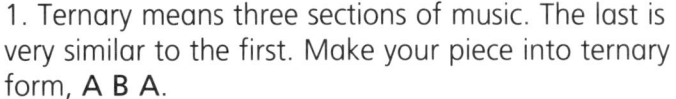

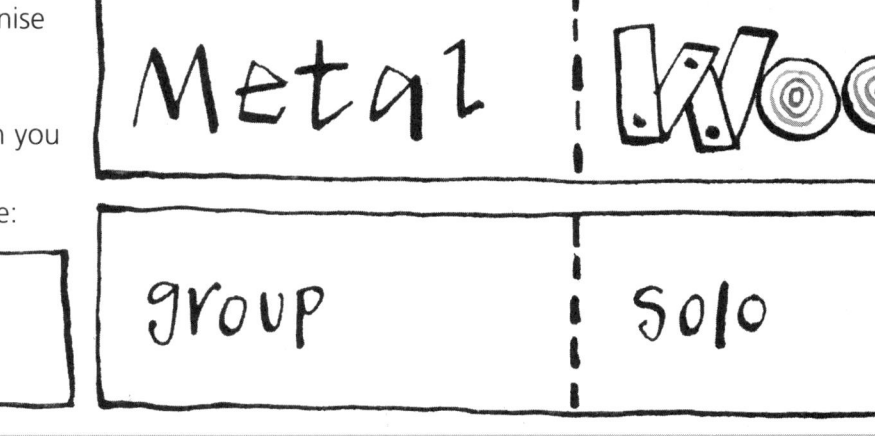

Second movement from Recorder concerto

What you need to know about the music

Composer: Antonio Vivaldi (1678–1741)

Vivaldi was one of the most important composers of the baroque period. He was nicknamed the 'Red Priest' because of his red hair and because he trained as a priest. Many of his compositions featured his own instrument, the violin, but he wrote concertos for many other instruments, including this one for treble recorder.

Features of the music

• Vivaldi wrote this as a chamber concerto, meaning that it was for a small group of instruments – a treble recorder (the **solo** instrument), two violins, one cello, and harpsichord. There are three movements in all; the first and last are at a lively tempo (*allegro*) and the middle movement featured here is slow (*largo*). The minor key of the music along with the slow pace gives the second movement a melancholy but lyrical mood.

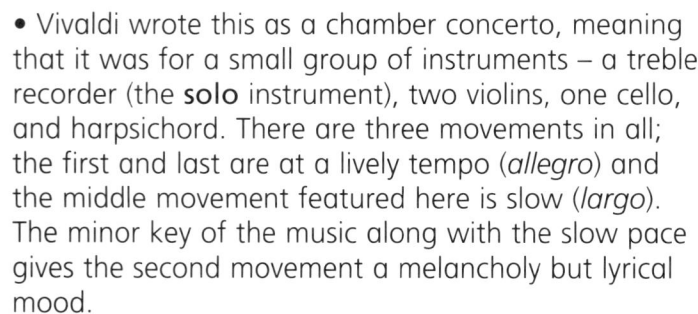

cello and harpsichord continuo

Accompaniment pattern

• The harpsichord and cello play the continuo (see page 29) and set the speed by playing on each beat to a slow count of three (**track 24**):

         1   2   3   1   2   3   etc

• The two violins add rising and falling patterns.

This accompaniment pattern continues throughout.

violins

Solo recorder

• After the accompaniment pattern is heard on its own, the solo recorder begins a slow, flowing melody.

• Long, smooth phrases are decorated with –

     fast rising runs of notes
     trills (next-door notes rapidly alternated)

recorder

Activity 1

class

Concerto dance

The children will listen to the music, responding in body movements to:

     the accompaniment group
     the solo recorder.

They will work in small groups to devise dances which reflect the structure and mood of the music.

What you will need
– space to move, eg a hall
– track 25

What to do
Devising the accompaniment dance movements

Listen to track 25 Second movement from Recorder concerto

Ask the children to focus their listening on the accompaniment instruments.

Questions you might ask
What do you notice about the music these instruments play? (It is slow and regular. It doesn't change. The violins play a rising and falling pattern which keeps repeating. The harpsichord and cello play on the counts –
1   2   3   1   2   3.)

Play the music again, asking the children to try out some simple movements which they can perform as a group, over and over again in a circle. Ask individual children to demonstrate and discuss their ideas. Which do they think match the music most closely?

• Divide the class into circles of five or six. Each group will choose one movement idea to perform during the music, eg

– facing around the circle; three forward steps on 1 2 3, pause for three counts, three forward steps, etc

– kneeling, facing outwards, hands on shoulders and swaying in unison from right to left on 1 2 3.

Devising the solo dance movements

Listen to track 25 Second movement from Recorder concerto

Focus on the recorder melody.

Questions you might ask
What do you notice about the recorder melody? (It is smooth. It does not repeat in a pattern. It is mostly slow but there are some fast decorations. It uses low and high notes, sometimes moving higher very quickly.)

One child per group will be the soloist. The soloists will listen carefully to the recorder melody as they improvise movements which will reflect the shapes of the music.

• Solo movement ideas
– lead up and down with alternate hands, elbows, arms
– turn at different speeds, responding to the music
– flutter hands to match shakes and trills.

Combining the solo and accompaniment movements

• Each soloist dances in the centre of a circle of accompaniment dancers. While the accompaniment group performs its repeating dance to the accompaniment music, the soloist improvises a freer dance, responding to the recorder melody.

What to assess

Discuss the links between the soloist's movements and the recorder melody.
Did the accompaniment group move together and keep in time with the music?

Listening links

What you need to know about the music

Canzona super entrada aechiopicam

Composer: Samuel Scheidt (1587–1654)

A canzona was originally a song for several voices, but in the 16th and 17th centuries it became a popular instrumental form featuring overlapping melodies and imitation (one instrument copying another).

This canzona for two cornetts and four sackbuts with a chamber organ continuo (hardly noticeable) is based on an old popular melody. It is played first by one cornett, imitated at a higher pitch by second cornett, at a lower pitch by the sackbut, then by the even lower bass sackbut. In between, the instruments overlap in a seamless texture. (Staff notation page 77.)

Recorder concerto

Composer: Antonio Vivaldi (1678–1741)

The first and last movements of the *Recorder concerto* are fast (*allegro*) in contrast with the slow (*largo*) middle movement. The harpsichord and cello play a continuo accompaniment while the recorder and two violins play as though in a lively conversation.

Chorus from The hunt cantata

Composer: Johann Sebastian Bach (1685–1750)

This cantata (page 29) was composed to celebrate the birthday of a Duke, a keen huntsman, at the court where Bach was employed. The singers are two sopranos (high female), tenor (high male) and bass (low male). They enter in turn from the highest to lowest voice with the first melody – an upward leap followed by a falling run of notes. The small orchestra of strings, oboes, bassoon and harpsichord then repeat this treatment of the melody, and horns add decoration and a hunting atmosphere.

Track 26 — Canzona super entrada aechiopicam

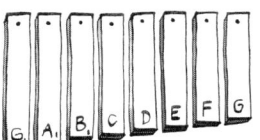

Work in pairs or small groups

What you will need

Tuned instruments – notes G A B C' D' E' F' G'

This piece is based on an old popular song. It is played by two cornetts and four sackbuts.

1. Play this short melody before you listen to the piece.

1	2	3	4	**1**	2	3	4
C	G.	C		C	B. A. G.		

Now listen to the canzona. The composer uses the same melody.

2. Listen to how the instruments copy each other. This is called imitation.

Try playing the melody in imitation. Use this diagram to see when to play.

1	2	3	4	**1**	2	3	4	**1**	2	3	4
player 1 begins											
C	G.	C		C	B. A. G.						
player 2 imitates player 1											
	C	G.	C		C	B. A. G.					
player 3 imitates player 2											
		C	G.	C		C	B. A. G.				

3. Play the melody on notes D E F G.

Play it together and then in imitation.

1	2	3	4	**1**	2	3	4	**1**	2	3	4
G	D	G		G	F E D						
	G	D	G		G	F E D					

4. Listen to the *Canzona* again. Focus on the other melodies the composer uses in between repeats of the first one. Can you sing along with them?

5. Make up some new melodies of your own to play in between.

6. Now organise your canzona. Decide when you will play the first melody together, when in imitation, and when you will add your new melodies.

Photocopiable worksheet

Track 27   *Recorder concerto*

Work in pairs. You will hear two extracts – they are the openings of the first and last movements of Vivaldi's recorder concerto. They are both called *Allegro*, which means fast.

What you will need
One instrument each.

What to do
1. Listen to both extracts.
The violins and the recorder are taking it in turns to play as if they are having a lively conversation.

2. Listen again. This time concentrate on the cello and harpsichord. Discuss what they are playing. Are they included in the conversation at all, or do they always play an accompaniment?

3. Use your own instruments to have a musical conversation with your partner. Listen to your partner's playing and reply in sounds.

How can you show when you are impatient, happy, cross, tired, arguing, agreeing?

```
4.
```

4. Compare these two extracts with track 25 – the slow middle movement. Does the recorder have a conversation with the other instruments in track 25?

5. Invent dances with your partner which show the conversation between the violins and the recorder in the *Allegros*.

Track 28   *Chorus from The hunt cantata*

This music is for voices and a small orchestra. It is from a cantata by the composer, Johann Sebastian Bach. The words are in German – Bach's language. They are about the Roman goddess of hunting, Diana, and they say:

Shine brightly, Aurora, as Diana keeps watch on the heavens by night, as the forests flower, shine brightly!

```
1.
```

1. Listen to the music and concentrate on the voices. How does Bach organise the melody? (Clue: do the singers start singing all at once or take it in turns?)

2. How many singers are there and how do their voices sound – high, low, in-between?

```
2.
```

3. Can you hear any of these instruments? Draw a circle round those you can hear and name them.

_____ and _____

4. Listen again. Do you hear any other instruments? Circle the ones you hear.

```
4.   bassoon     xylophone     drum

     oboe     piano          horn
```

5. Compare the start of the singers' music with the start of the instruments on their own. What is the same? What is different?

```
5.
```

Classical

The emphasis in architecture and music during the 18th century was on grace and beauty, balanced proportions and formal structure. The elaborately-decorated buildings and music of the baroque period were gradually followed by much simpler and clearer designs. In all kinds of music, strong melody lines became the outstanding feature.

New ways of structuring music emerged. The most important of these was sonata form (see page 42), which was used to structure all kinds of music during the classical period, including the individual movements (separate sections) of orchestral, solo and small group pieces.

The symphony was established as a large scale work for orchestra, with first three, then later four separate movements of contrasting speeds and character.

The orchestra expanded in size and range of instruments during this time, particularly in the woodwind section which now began to include the newly-invented clarinet. In addition to a larger string section, the classical orchestra frequently combined flutes, oboes, bassoons and horns. As the orchestra grew in strength, the use of the harpsichord continuo as a supporting background gradually stopped.

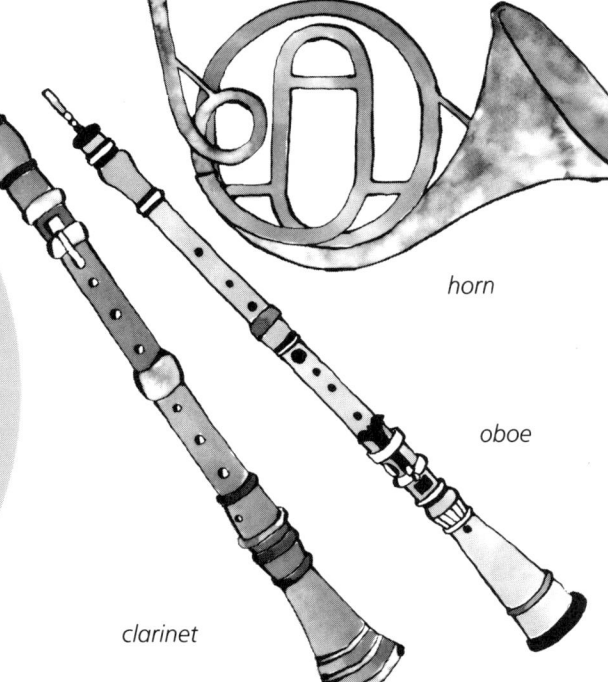

horn

oboe

clarinet

First movement from The 'hen' symphony by Joseph Haydn

This is one of over a hundred symphonies Haydn composed. By the end of the classical period the organisation of a symphony into four contrasting movements had become standard, and Haydn's selection of movements for this one was typical of the time. He marked them:

1. Allegro (fast) 2. Andante (slow)
3. Menuet (a dance)
4. Vivace (fast)

Classical composers wrote vocal music for the church, but opera held a greater fascination. The elaborate staging and special effects of earlier operas became less important than dramatic content as composers developed characters and plots to comment on aspects of human nature.

In England, the 17th century Puritans had regarded Christmas as a superstition, and their continuing influence meant that from 1700 to 1782 the only Christmas carol accepted by the Church of England was 'While shepherds watched'. There remains, however, a wealth of carols from the Nonconformist repertoire.

Ein Mädchen oder Weibchen
by Wolfgang Amadeus Mozart

Mozart's opera, The Magic Flute, written at the end of his short life, is one of his most successful and popular operas, often performed today. Ein Mädchen oder Weibchen is an aria – a song. It is written for male voice and is accompanied by an orchestra, including a glockenspiel. The German text humorously describes the plight of the comic character, Papageno, the birdcatcher, in his search for a wife.

A Christmas carol
by Caleb Ashworth

This is a Nonconformist Christmas carol for voices in three parts. It would have been sung in English country parish churches.

First movement from The 'hen' symphony

What you need to know about the music

Composer: Joseph Haydn (1732–1809)

Haydn's father was a wheelwright, but Haydn had already shown a talent for music by the time he was eight, when the organist of Vienna's cathedral heard him sing and recruited him into the choir. Later, he became director of music for the Prince of Esterhazy and his family. During the thirty years he stayed with them, his enormous output of music was published and his reputation spread throughout Europe.

Features of the music

The 'hen' symphony (composed in 1785) is one of Haydn's six 'Paris symphonies', commissioned for a Parisian orchestra. It was nicknamed 'La poule' (the hen) because of the clucking oboe part in the first movement. The orchestra contains:

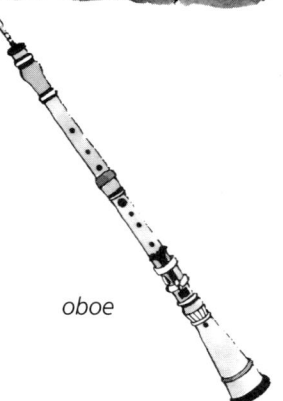

oboe

    1 flute
    2 oboes,
    2 bassoons
    2 horns
    strings (violins, violas, cellos, double basses)

The first movement is in a structure called sonata form, which has clearly identifiable sections:

Exposition
The composer presents (exposits) the musical ideas on which the whole movement is based. They are grouped within a *first subject* followed by a *second subject*.

Development
The musical ideas of the exposition are developed.

Recapitulation
The exposition is played again (recapitulated).

Coda – ending.

Activity 1

CLASS

1st idea 2nd idea etc

Hen chant (exposition)

As a class, the children will learn a rhythmic chant based on the six musical ideas Haydn used for his first and second subjects. The chant forms the exposition of a new piece in sonata form which they will create.

What to do

• First teach the class to say the whole chant (**track 29** will help you). When it is secure, divide into six groups and perform it again, each group saying one idea.

1st subject

Jo – seph Hay – dn and a **hen** and a **hen** and a **hen,**   Jo – seph Hay – dn and a **hen** and a **hen** and a **hen.**

2nd subject

What a hen what a **chick**-en what a hen what a **chick**-en, **and** that Jo – seph Hay – dn how he **makes** her **cluck**

chicka chicka **chick**a chicka **chick**

Photocopiable chant

42

Activity 2

Developing musical ideas

The children play a class circle game in preparation for Activity 3 in which they will plan a development section for *The hen chant*. The game puts Haydn's musical ideas into a new unplanned order, and also explores the effect of unplanned changes in dynamics, pitch, texture and timbre; all are ways of developing ideas.

What to do

• Each child secretly chooses whether to be *Joseph Haydn* or a *hen*. The children say their words out loud in turn, giving the musical ideas a new order:

• Repeat, but this time, ask the children each secretly to decide whether to say the words loudly or quietly.

• Now each secretly decides on a way to vary their vocal timbre and pitch, eg saying the words in a scratchy hen-like, high-pitched voice.

• The texture might be varied by appointing a conductor to bring the children in one, two, three or more at a time.

• At each stage, consider the effectiveness of these unplanned changes. Which effects do the children feel work well? Which would they like to adopt in a planned development?

Activity 3

Hen chant development

Developing the first subject

• Ask the two, original *Joseph Haydn* and *hen* groups (Activity 1) to decide on an effective development of their two musical ideas. This will form part of a larger development section. They should decide on order, dynamics, timbre, pitch and texture and find a way to write all this down so that they can remember it.

Developing the second subject

• The four, second subject groups (Activity 1) try out and decide on a way of developing their musical ideas, again considering the effectiveness of order, dynamics, timbre, pitch, and texture, and drawing a final plan.

Developing both subjects together

• Now all six groups find a way to develop effectively the musical ideas from both subjects.

Completing the development

• Finally, decide on an order in which to perform these three separate sections to make a complete development. Make a large plan for everyone to see, eg

1st subject	2nd subject	1st subject	Both	2nd subject

What to assess

What do the children think of the development? Does the order feel right? Is it too long/too short? Is the texture too simple, too complex? Are changes in dynamics, timbre and pitch clear? Is the performance neat or untidy – do they need a conductor? (One child might tap a steady beat to keep the chant rhythmical.)

Activity 4

Hen chant in sonata form

The class now performs the chant in sonata form:

Exposition
All together, perform the chant as in Activity 1.

Development
Perform the complete development devised in Activity 3.

Recapitulation
All perform the chant as in Activity 1 again.

Coda
Choose an ending, eg all together say very loudly 'What a hen!'

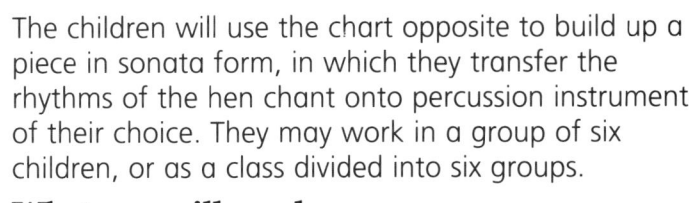
Listen to track 31 First movement from
The 'hen' symphony

Focus the children's listening on the first and second subject ideas, which will be familiar to them from the hen chant (Activity 1). Note that the ideas are repeated many times (the chant is simplified). Can they identify the six musical ideas within the two subjects?

Next, ask the children to identify the beginning of each main section of the sonata form: exposition, development, recapitulation, coda. (The description below and **track 30** will help you locate them yourself.)

Exposition

First subject – the two ideas, *Joseph Haydn* and *and a hen*, are played several times by violins and flutes.

Link (ending with a falling run of short, crisp notes played on violins) leads to –

Second subject – the violins play the bouncy *what a hen what a chicken* idea, then the oboes cluck *chicka chicka chick*.

Development

The first subject is immediately followed by the violins playing the second subject, then it is combined with the flutes clucking *chicka chicka chick*.

The four-note rising *Joseph Haydn* idea of the first subject is played forcefully by different combinations of strings and woodwind. The idea is repeated many times at different pitches and combined with energetic running patterns.

Recapitulation

First subject – reappears briefly.

Link – the key changes from minor to major (a brighter sound) then the falling run leads to

Second subject in the major key with flutes clucking *chicka chicka chick*.

The music is interrupted by a pause, a long, held note, then –

Coda

The violins play the clucking idea for the last time.

Activity 5

Hen instrumental in sonata form

The children will use the chart opposite to build up a piece in sonata form, in which they transfer the rhythms of the hen chant onto percussion instruments of their choice. They may work in a group of six children, or as a class divided into six groups.

What you will need
– copies of the chart for each of the six groups/individuals
– a range of instruments from which to choose six, eg

maraca

tambour

guiro

gato drum

woodblock

rattle

What to do
The children will decide how many times to play the first and second subject ideas, how to develop the ideas, recapitulate them and bring their piece to an end. They will need to fill in the chart to show the order.

What to assess
Let the groups perform their compositions to the class. Is the structure of the pieces clear – can each section of the sonata form be identified by the listeners now that there are no words to help? Have the children made good use of the instruments – playing loudly and quietly, changing them, combining them?

Hen instrumental

Use Haydn's musical ideas to make a new piece of instrumental music in sonata form.

Work in sixes – six groups or six people – one to each musical idea. Select a different percussion instrument for each idea.

Exposition

Decide on order for the musical ideas. This doesn't have to be the one chosen by Haydn. You decide. Use the space opposite to record your order.

Development

Develop your ideas by re-ordering them, playing them louder or quieter, changing the instrument, or combining them in different ways. Record the new order in the space.

Recapitulation

(repeat of exposition) Use this space to remind yourselves of any small changes to the exposition.

Coda

Decide how to end your piece, and record it here.

Exposition

Development

Recapitulation

Coda

A Christmas carol

What you need to know about the music

Composer: Caleb Ashworth

In 1762, Caleb Ashworth published 'A collection of tunes' which were 'designed for those who have made some Proficiency in the Art of Singing'. Only about one in ten country churches had an organ by 1800, so at this time rural choirs sang unaccompanied or with small bands of instrumentalists.

Features of the music

This carol is for soprano (high), tenor (middle) and bass (low) voices. Like many Nonconformist hymns the melody is sandwiched between a descant (high part), and a bass (low) part. In some verses both the descant and the melody are sung by soprano and tenor voices at their own pitch.

Each verse has a different musical texture. A bassoon plays along with the bass voice in all verses.

Verse 1	Verse 2	Verse 3	Verse 4
Descant soprano/tenor		**Descant** tenor	**Descant** soprano/tenor
Melody soprano/tenor	**Melody** soprano	**Melody** soprano	**Melody** soprano/tenor
Bass	**Bass**	**Bass**	**Bass**

Activity 1   Singing A Christmas carol

The children will learn to sing the carol melody then accompany it with a simplified version of the bass line. (Staff notation on page 77 for music readers.) They will consider **texture** in arranging a final performance.

What you will need

– copies of the songsheet, bass line and **track 32** and **33**
– low-pitched tuned instruments, eg bass xylophone, keyboard, with notes – **G₁ C D E G**

What to do

• Teach the melody to the whole class using the recording of the first verse on **track 32**. You might listen to it several times, then join in singing the first two lines, then all four. Finally sing all four verses.

• Choose a small group of instrumentalists to work out and play the bass line (**track 33**). When they are confident, ask them to play it to the class.

• If using tuned percussion, use two beaters and roll (play alternate hands very quickly) the 3-count notes to create a continuous sound:

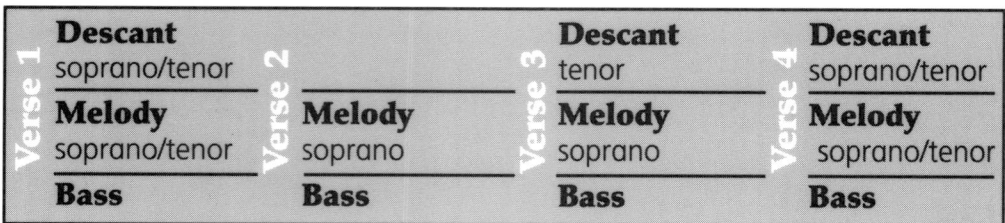

```
1  2  3  1  2  3  1  2  3  1  2  3
G......  E......  E  C  D  G......
```

Listen to track 34 A Christmas carol

Listen to the verses one by one, and ask the children to focus on:

– the melody in verse 1
– the bass line in verse 2
– any extra part/s in verse 3
– what happens in verse 4

Questions you might ask
Did you recognise any of the parts? (The melody was the same as the one we sang. Our bass line was similar but their basses sang extra notes.) What else did you notice? (There is another melody, sung above the melody we learned. It was sung in verses 1, 3 and 4. In verse 4 there were more voices than in verse 2 and 3. Verse 4 was the same as verse 1.)

• Now perform the melody with the bass line.

• Ask the children for ways to vary the textures of each verse, eg 1. solo voice and bass, 2. three voices with bass, 3. all voices no bass, 4. all voices with bass.

What to assess

Are the singers and instrumentalists combining well? Does the volume of the accompaniment complement the different textures chosen for each verse?

A Christmas carol

1. Let an anthem of praise and a carol of joy
   Each tongue and each heart in sweet concert employ:
   This day sprung at Beth'lem a plant of renown,
   And Christ to redeem us abandoned a crown.

2. Conceived of a virgin! How humble his birth
   Not graced with the pomp and the grandeur of earth
   But laid in a manger, with beasts, at an Inn;
   No room for the Saviour of Israel within!

3. The shepherds with pleasure saluted the morn
   When Jesus, the Shepherd of Judah, was born;
   The sages with wonder acknowledged his star
   And brought him their homage and gifts from afar.

4. Great Saviour, the tribute of honour we pay
   And celebrate gladly this festival day:
   We triumph in Britain thy glory to see;
   Not sages nor shepherds more happy than we.

Bass line grid

Play the bass line on a low-sounding instrument. Use the note grid or music notation to learn the notes.

count in   1   2   3   1   2   Let an

1 2 3	1 2 3	1 2 3	1 2 3
G	E	E C D	G͵
an – them of	praise and a	ca – rol of	joy each
G	E	E C D	G͵
tongue and each	heart in sweet	con – cert em–	ploy: This
D	G͵	G	D
day sprung at	Beth' – lem a	plant of re –	nown And
C E D		E C D	G͵
Christ to re –	deem us a –	ban – doned a	crown.
1 2 3	1 2 3	1 2 3	1 2 3

Ein Mädchen oder Weibchen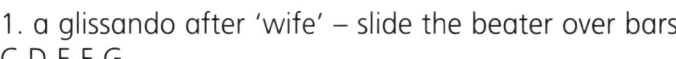

What you need to know about the music

Composer: Wolfgang Amadeus Mozart

(1756–91)

This aria (song) comes from Mozart's comic opera, *The Magic Flute*, which he composed in the last year of his life. It was commissioned by the owner of a popular theatre near Vienna who wrote the German libretto (opera script). Despite his failing health Mozart conducted from the fortepiano (early piano) at the first performance in September 1791. It immediately become one of his most popular operas.

Features of the music

The comic character, Papageno the birdcatcher, accompanies Tamino on a quest through enchanted lands to release an imprisoned princess with the aid of a magic flute and bells. Papageno, however, is also on a quest of his own and in the aria *Ein Mädchen oder Weibchen* ('a maiden or a wife') describes his search for a wife. The aria is accompanied by the orchestra and features a glockenspiel as the magic bells.

Listen to track 35 Ein Mädchen oder Weibchen

Explain that the children will hear Papageno's song sung in German, Mozart's language. Ask them to notice the magic bell sounds.

Questions you might ask
At the beginning the magic bells play a melody with the orchestra. What do you notice about this melody? (It is the same as the first melody sung by Papageno – an introduction.)
Do you hear the bells play when Papageno sings? (No, but they play short patterns in-between the lines of his song.)
When do the bells play on their own and what do they play? (Before Papageno sings a second melody the bells play the first part of it as an introduction.)
What happens after Papageno sings the second melody. (The whole thing is repeated; there are different words.)
Which classroom instrument sounds like the magic bells? (Glockenspiel.)

Activity 1

Singing an aria

The children sing an English version of the aria with a simple accompaniment.

What you will need
– copies of the song sheet and **track 36**
– finger cymbals, bells, or bell tree
– glockenspiel notes C D E F G and a small hard beater

• What to do
Teach the children the English version of the song using **track 36** and the song sheet opposite. (A simple piano accompaniment can be found on page 78.)

• Accompaniment
Ask individual children to devise a rhythmic accompaniment for the song, using finger cymbals, jingle bells or a bell tree. Try out their ideas while the rest of the class sing the song.

1.

2.

• Magic bell glissando – fast slide of notes
Now add these glockenspiel sounds to the song:

1. a glissando after 'wife' – slide the beater over bars C D E F G.

2. a glissando after 'life' – bars C D E F.

What to assess
Are the instrumentalists able to play confidently in time without interrupting the flow of the singing?

Activity 2

Compose a magic spell

In groups the children devise magic spell music to play between repeats of the aria. (See worksheet opposite.) A final performance may need a conductor to bring the different groups in at the appropriate times.

Singing an aria
O maiden come to join me

O maiden come to join me,

be Papageno's wife,

A turtle dove beside me,

that's all I want of life!

Each day would be feasting and

    pleasure

I'd envy no monarch his treasure

And that's all the wisdom I need

My life would be heaven indeed!

Photocopiable song sheet

Compose magic spell music

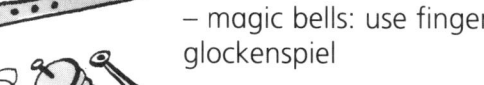

Work in groups.

What you will need

– a magic flute: use panpipes, recorder, whistles

– magic bells: use finger cymbals, jingle bells, glockenspiel

– any other soundmakers you think sound magical (try some special effects on keyboard)

What to do

Sit in a circle. Decide which instrument each player will use.

1. Listen to your sounds one by one around the circle.

2. Listen to your sounds in pairs – which pairs do you like?

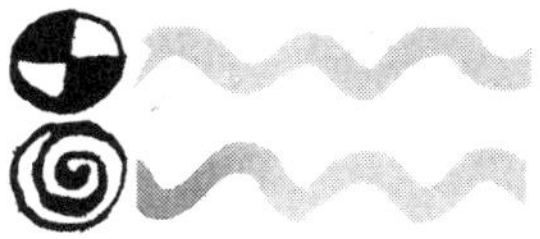

3. Listen to your sounds overlapping. Each player joins in one at a time.

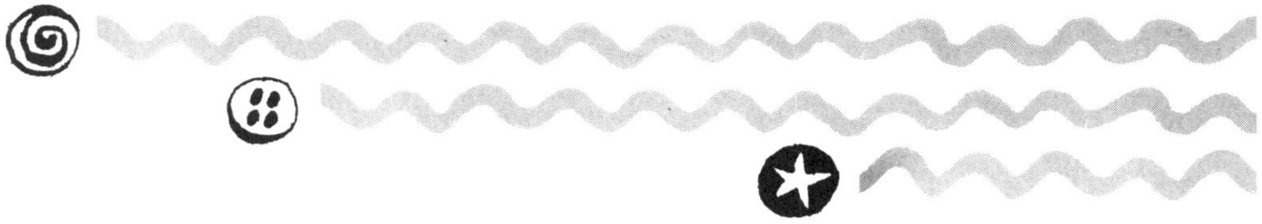

4. Now begin to organise some magic spell music. Decide which sounds you will use and how you will start and end your piece. Do you need a conductor? Or do you need to draw or write a plan of your piece to help you remember what you have decided?

Now perform the spell music. The class sings the aria once, then you play, then the class sings again.

Photocopiable worksheet

Listening links

What you need to know about the music

Second movement from The 'hen' symphony

Composer: Joseph Haydn (1732-1809)

This extract is the opening of the second movement. Listen for these features:

- a smooth, quiet melody on the strings
- a falling phrase on woodwind leading to a repeat
- conversation between violins and cellos with a new melody
- two loud, fast falling runs of notes
- a regular 'clucking' getting quieter and quieter
- sudden loud burst of sound by the whole orchestra.

Pastorale

Composer: Pieter Hellendaal (1721 - 99)

Hellendaal was a Dutch composer, violinist and organist, who studied in Italy then lived and worked in England.

Pastorale is from his violin concerto (1758). It depicts the scene around the crib in Bethlehem as the shepherds play bagpipes to the baby Jesus. *Pastorale* was the term for a popular type of music of the period in which an idealised vision of the countryside was portrayed in gentle, lilting rhythms, often with drones (page 6) imitating the sound of bagpipes. Hellendaal's orchestra consists of strings, woodwind and harpsichord.

Variations on Ein Mädchen oder Weibchen

Composer: Ludwig van Beethoven (1770-1827)

In 1797, six years after the first performance of *The Magic Flute*, Beethoven composed twelve variations for cello and piano on 'Ein Mädchen oder Weibchen'. You will hear:
- Theme – on piano with cello accompaniment
- Variation 2 theme on cello with piano accompaniment
- Variation 4 parts of theme on cello, piano answers.

Track 37 Second movement – The 'hen' symphony

This is the second movement from *The 'hen' symphony* by Haydn. Listen to it and compare it with the first movement.

1. What differences do you notice?

> 1.

2. What are the similarities?

> 2.

3. Does anything still remind you of the hen in the title?

> 3.

4. How does Haydn use the orchestra to surprise us in this piece?

What happens just before the surprise? Why do you think Haydn does this?

> 4.

5. Listen to the second movement several times then draw a diagram or picture of the way the music changes during the movement.

> 5.

Photocopiable worksheet

Track 38   Pastorale

Work in pairs.

This music describes the sounds of the shepherds' bagpipes as they welcome the baby Jesus in his crib in the stable at Bethlehem.

The first sound you hear is a drone - a long low note which is played all the time. Bagpipes play a drone and here the composer imitates their sound. Have you heard a drone before?

Listen carefully to the melody. After every short melody there is a quiet echo.

Play the echo game

What to do

1. Choose two untuned instruments, eg tambourines. Play a short rhythm for your partner to echo quietly.

Keep the game going with a different rhythm each time. Can your partner always echo the pattern or is it sometimes too long or complicated to remember?

2. Swap over so you both have a turn at playing the echo.

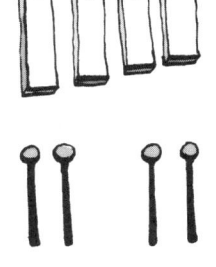

3. Now choose a tuned instrument to share, eg xylophone. Use one set of beaters each.

Play the game again, this time making up short tunes. Start with only 3 or 4 notes in each tune. How long can you make your melodies and still echo them accurately?

Photocopiable worksheet

Track 39   Variations

Listen to the music. You will hear three different sections: a melody followed by two variations (different versions).

1. How many instruments are playing? What are they?

> 1.

2. Do you recognise the melody? Which opera is it from and who is it by?

> 2.

Now listen several times to answer these questions.

3. Which instrument plays the melody in the first and second sections of the music?

> 3.

4. Describe what happens in the third section. Is this the same melody? Can you say how it has changed?

> 4.

5. Sing *Ein Mädchen oder Weibchen*. Now think of two ways to change it to make two variations.

Here are some ideas, but you may have others.

- sing it in a quiet voice making all the notes short
- play the rhythm of the words on a triangle
- sing it with a rhythmic accompaniment on bells

Perform your theme and two variations to the class.

Photocopiable worksheet

51

Romantic

c1820–c1900

At the end of the 18th century, writers, painters and philosophers began to explore new ways of expressing human emotion. These new 'romantic' ideals were soon adopted by composers, who began to make their music describe feelings and moods, pictures and stories, mystery and adventure. They freed themselves from the formal structures of the classical period and allowed the content or ideas of the composition to determine the structure.

They used more colourful, and often larger combinations of instruments. The range of the orchestra was extended by adding lower-pitched instruments such as bass clarinet and tuba, and higher-pitched instruments such as piccolo.

Public concerts and musical evenings, soirées, in the home became a regular feature of social life for the middle classes. The patronage of the very wealthy, which had sustained composers and musicians in earlier times became less significant. The demand for large- and small-scale music came from a much more public audience. Music-making in the home consisted of songs, piano pieces, and chamber music (music for a small group). Composers wrote pieces for a wide variety of instrumental combinations, often according to the requirements of particular players.

Theme and variations
from The 'trout' quintet
by Franz Schubert

In 1819 Schubert was commissioned by a wealthy mine owner and amateur cellist, Sylvester Paumgartner, to write a piece of music for piano, violin, viola, cello and double bass, which were the instruments which he and his friends could play.

The work includes a set of variations on Schubert's song, 'The trout', and the whole quintet (piece for five players) is recognised as one of his finest works.

The piano became a very important solo instrument in the 19th century, and an enormous quantity of music was composed for it in the romantic style. Several technical developments to its construction were made, which gave the piano more notes and a wider range of volume and tone.

Polka
by Alexander Borodin

This takes a well-known musical exercise for children as a starting point for a piano piece in the style of a lively dance, the polka. The piece became so popular that other Russian composers, including Nikolay Rimsky-Korsakov, used the same idea in a collection of pieces for piano, and Franz Liszt composed a short prelude to play before it.

Exhilarating new dances appeared in the 19th century ballrooms of Europe. Both the waltz and polka were partner dances which developed from regional folk dances and became so popular that they were used by composers for concert music as well as in the ballroom.

With the rise of industrialisation and an increase in affluence, many moderately wealthy families bought pianos and enjoyed music-making in the home. While the virtuoso composer/performer was the star of the concert hall and salon, a huge repertoire of music was also becoming available to the amateur player.

Waltz
from Serenade for strings
by Peter Ilyich Tchaikovsky

This piece of orchestral concert music is also based on a dance. The waltz achieved the height of its popularity in Vienna and swept through Europe to the exclusion of almost every other dance. At the first performance of the Serenade in Moscow in 1881 it was the Waltz, second of the four movements, which the enthusiastic audience demanded as an encore.

53

Theme and variations from The 'trout' quintet

What you need to know about the music

Composer: Franz Schubert (1797–1828)

Franz Schubert was born in Vienna, a great musical centre in his day. He was taught the violin by his schoolmaster father, a keen amateur musician, and the piano by his elder brother. In 1808 he became a choirboy and began a formal musical education.

He composed 600 songs in his short lifetime, writing the first as a teenager. In 1819, two years after composing a song called *The trout*, he reused the song's melody in a quintet (piece for five musicians) commissioned by a wealthy, amateur cellist.

The 'trout' quintet has five movements (separate sections). The fourth is a set of variations based on the melody of the song. The theme (melody) and four of the six variations (1, 2, 3, 5) are explored here.

Features of the music

- The instruments used are:

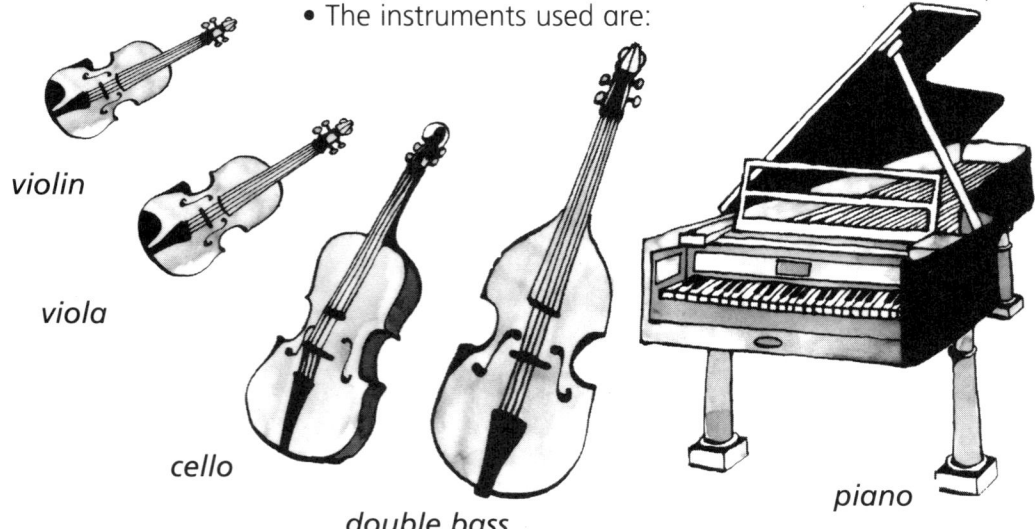

violin

viola

cello

double bass

piano

- The diagram opposite shows when the instruments are used and some features of the music they play.

	Melody 🐟	Accompaniment
Theme	violin plays the melody	viola and cello — bass
Var 1 (first variation of the theme)	pianist plays the melody with both hands, adding decorations	violin, viola, cello play gently up and down waves, then high-pitched ripples on violin; bass moves up and down in jumps plucking the strings
Var 2	viola, cello, bass play melody at medium–low pitch; piano echoes part of the melody	violin plays fast running notes high above the melody
Var 3	cello and bass play the melody jauntily at low pitch	violin and viola play crisp, rhythm patterns until two smoother patterns at the end; piano plays very fast and joyful up and down waves and runs of notes
Var 5	gentle, smooth version of melody played by cello in minor key	violin and viola play gentle undulations; bass plays spiky jumps; piano enters half way with chord 'bubbles', moving up and down in opposite directions

Activity 1 — Reading a score – the theme

Class

The children will follow the graphic score, listening to the melody of the song (theme) and familiarising themselves with the sounds of the instruments as the melody is played by one then others in each of the variations.

What you will need
– one enlarged copy of the score (pages 58–9) for the whole class to follow, and a copy for each child

Before photocopying the pages, you will need to cover up some lines with masking tape so that the copies may be used for activity 3. Cover:
var 1 – violin/viola/cello line; var 2 – violin line;
var 3 – violin/viola line; var 5 – piano line

Listen to track 40 Theme and variations from The 'trout' quintet

Listen to the *Theme* and *Variations 1, 2, 3* and *5*. The fish motif indicates the melody, and shows which instruments play it. As they listen (more than once if necessary) to the theme then each variation one at a time, follow the melody and notice the change of instruments on the score.

Questions you might ask.
Which instrument plays the melody first? (The violin.)
In Variation 1, do you notice anything different about the way the melody is played on the piano? (It sounds higher than it did when played on the violin, and wiggly decorations – trills – are added.)
What happens to the melody in Variation 2? (It is played by a group of instruments – violin, cello and bass – and the piano echoes parts of it.)
How does the melody change in Variation 3? (It is louder, more jerky and lower in pitch. It is played by cello and bass.)
Compare Variations 3 and 5. What is similar and what is different? (The melody is low-sounding in both but the moods are different. Variation 3 is lively and energetic; Variation 5 is smooth and sad.)

Activity 2 — Reading a score – accompaniment

Class

The children will listen to the music again, focussing this time on the way the accompaniment parts in each variation have been notated (those not masked).

Listen to track 40 Theme and variations from The 'trout' quintet

Look at the score with the children to discover which instruments to listen out for (Theme and Variations 1,2,3 and 5 only). After listening to the theme and each variation in turn, discuss the way the sounds have been notated, eg can the children hear the short, jumping bass notes in Variation 1 and see how these have been notated with jumping dots?

Activity 3 — Notating a score

The children will listen to the music, focussing on each accompaniment part which is masked in the score. As they listen, each child devises a way of notating the missing parts.

What you will need
– a copy of the score for each child

What to do
Remind the children of the attention they paid in Activity 2 to the way in which sounds have been notated in the score. Explain that they are now going to devise notations for the missing lines. You may prefer either to listen as a class or let individuals work at different times (listening frequently if necessary).

What to assess
When the children have completed their scores, discuss the results in small groups, comparing similarities and differences. Listen to the music again looking at a selection of children's notations and discussing their ideas. How appropriately do the notations represent the sounds? Compare with the unmasked suggestions.

Theme and variations from The 'trout' quintet

Reading a score – Notating a score

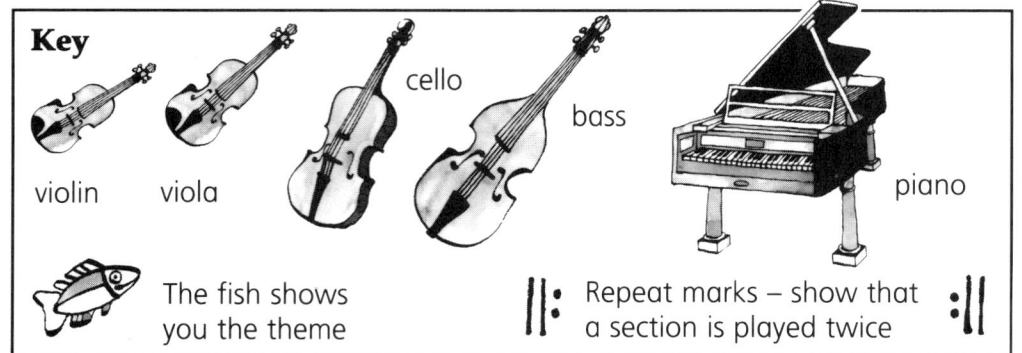

Key

violin   viola   cello   bass   piano

The fish shows you the theme

||: :|| Repeat marks – show that a section is played twice

Activity 1
Notice which instruments play the melody in each section.

Activity 2
Notice each of the parts opposite.

Activity 3
One part in the score is missing from each variation. Listen to each variation then draw the missing part.

Theme	
Var 1	
Var 2	
Var 3	
Var 5	

Theme

Variation 1

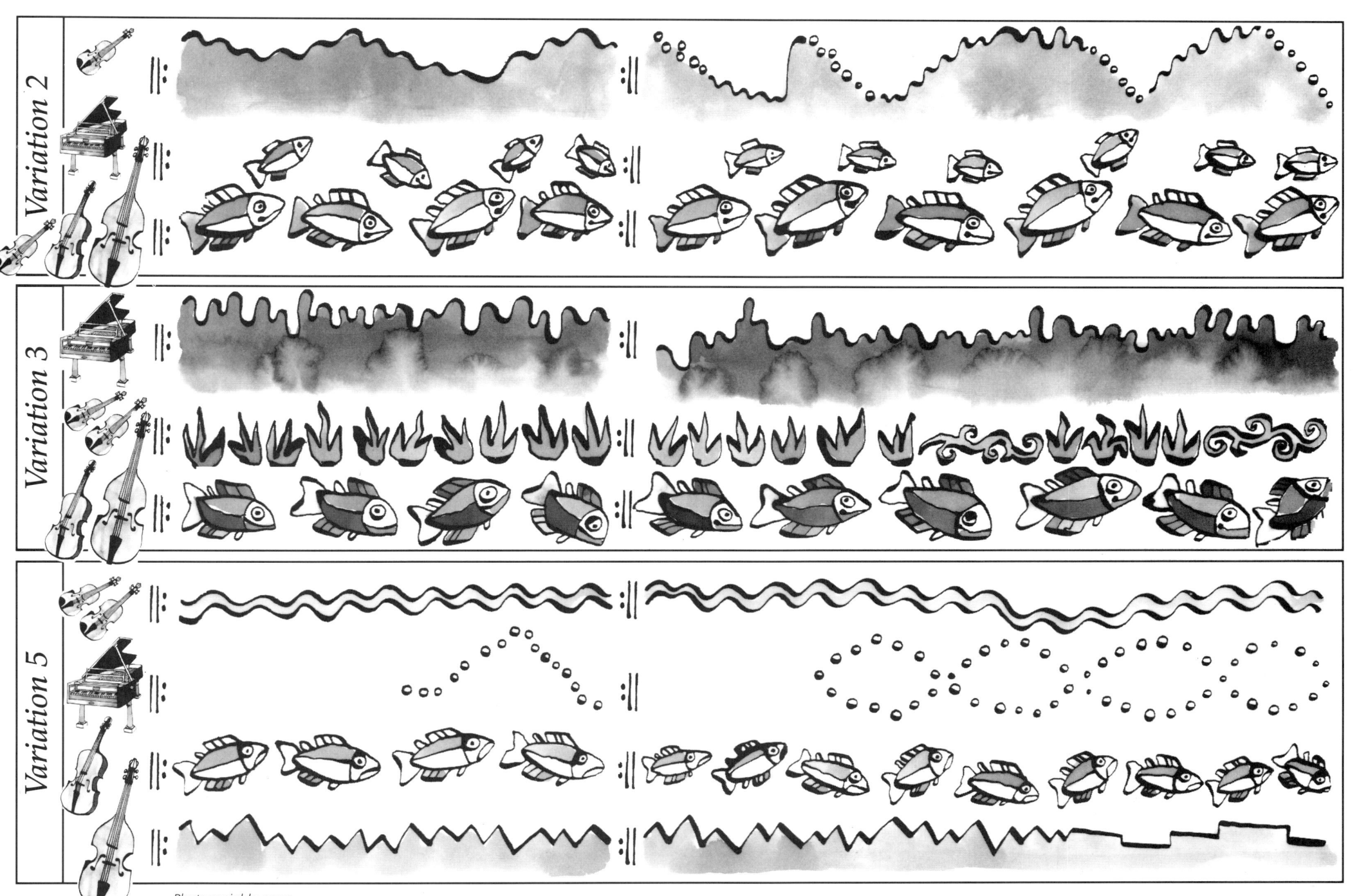

Photocopiable score

Polka

What you need to know about the music

Composer: Alexander Borodin (1833–87)

Borodin learned to play the flute and cello as a child and composed his first polka at the age of eight. However his other lifelong passion was for chemistry. Instead of becoming a full-time composer he trained in science and medicine and as an adult managed to compose music while following his main career. Much of his piano music was promoted throughout Western Europe by the virtuoso performer-composer, Franz Liszt, who travelled extensively giving concerts.

Features of the music

Polka is a piano duet (for two players). Borodin wrote it for himself and for his adopted daughter, Liza. Liza played the simple ostinato (repeated pattern) on which the whole piece is based.

This ostinato, often called 'Chopsticks', was a well-known piano exercise for children. The player uses one hand to play a pattern of notes which stretches the hand out from playing next-door notes to an octave (eight notes apart). It can also be played with the index fingers of both hands hence the name 'chopsticks'. Borodin added a lively set of simple melodies for the second player.

What to do

> ### Listen to track 41 Polka
>
> Focus the children's listening on the ostinato.
>
> *Questions you might ask*
> *What stays the same in this music? (A repeating pattern – ostinato – which is played many times all the way through.)*
> *What changes do you notice? (At the beginning the ostinato is played once slowly and quietly as an introduction, then it is repeated many times in a fast and lively way, while other melodies are played. At the end the ostinato is played twice, getting quieter and slower.)*

- Now let the children work out how to play the polka ostinato using the worksheet opposite (first half).
- Keyboard players may use the index fingers of both hands, or one hand and the fingers shown (right hand).
- Tuned percussionists should use two beaters, alternating left and right hands, to promote good co-ordination and a steady beat.

What to assess

Does the ostinato have an even, steady beat? Are the children able to play it over and over without a break between repeats? Have they the control to play quietly or loudly, quickly or slowly?

Activity 1

Playing the Polka ostinato

Individually, the children learn to play the Polka ostinato (**track 42**). Allow time for turns to be taken with instruments. (Staff notation on page 78.)

What you will need
– a copy of the worksheet opposite
– a keyboard or
– a xylophone with these notes: **C D E F G A B C'**

Activity 2

Composing a duet

Pairs of children use the ostinato as the basis for making up a new duet, featuring newly composed melodies, and expressive changes in dynamics and tempo.

What you will need
– a copy of the worksheet opposite
– a keyboard or xylophone with notes A,–C' including B♭ (and other sharps and flats if available)

What to do

Listen to track 41 Polka

Focus the children's listening on the other melodies in the Polka. Can the children sing any of them?

Questions you might ask
How long is each melody? (The same length as the ostinato pattern.)
Do any of them repeat? (Yes.)
Do they move at the same speed as the ostinato. (No, they have different, slower rhythms – one melody note for every two ostinato notes.)

• Using the second half of the worksheet opposite, the children work on composing a new duet. One child plays the ostinato while the other adds new, made up melodies. They should then swap.

• Some of Borodin's ideas are given. The children might use these to start with, but then think of some more of their own.

Preparing for a performance
The children need to:
• decide who will play the ostinato and who will add the melodies – perhaps they will take turns;
• decide on the order to add the new melodies;
• consider how tempo and dynamics might be used to change the character of the music;
• decide on how to co-ordinate tempo and dynamic changes. Discuss what might help (eg writing a plan of the music showing where changes take place; watching each other and giving pre-arranged signals; listening carefully to each other and responding to dynamic and speed changes in each other's playing.)
• practise enough to play confidently to the class.

What to assess
Have the children been able to make up new melodies which sound well with the ostinato? Have they considered tempo and dynamics? Are they able to carry out their intentions successfully in performance?

Playing the Polka ostinato

Use a keyboard or xylophone – listen to track 42.

Xylophone players
Use two beaters, alternating left (L) and right (R).

F	G	F	G	E	A	E	A	D	B	D	B	C	C'	C	C'
L	R	L	R	L	R	L	R	L	R	L	R	L	R	L	R

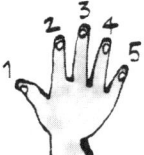

Keyboard players
Use both hands – index fingers only; or use right hand only and follow the finger numbers.

F	G	F	G	E	A	E	A	D	B	D	B	C	C'	C	C'
1	2	1	2	1	3	1	3	1	4	1	4	1	5	1	5

Composing a duet

With a partner use these notes to make up melodies to play with the ostinato. Here are some of Borodin's ideas to try first.

F	G	F	G	E	A	E	A	D	B	D	B	C	C'	C	C'
A,		B,		C				F				E			
A,				B♭,				B,				C			
A,		B,		C				B'				C'			
A,				B♭,				B♭,		B,		C			

Photocopiable worksheet

Waltz from Serenade for strings

What you need to know about the music

Composer: Peter Tchaikovsky (1840–93)

Tchaikovsky showed a keen interest in music as a child, and began piano lessons when he was four. Despite his ability in music he became a lawyer, but abandoned this career to become the successful composer of well-known works such as the *Nutcracker Ballet* and the *1812 Overture*.

The *Serenade for strings* was first performed in 1881 and has four movements (separate sections), the second of which is a waltz. It was a work of which Tchaikovsky was particularly fond. He used an orchestra consisting just of strings (violins, violas, cellos and basses); 'the more strings the better', he said. This gives a rich, smooth, romantic quality to the music.

Features of the music

The whole *Serenade* is built on the use of scales (a sequence of adjacent notes). The graceful waltz melody opens with a rising scale:

1	2	3	**1**	2	3	**1**	2	3	**1**	2	3
B♭	**C**	**D**	**E**	**F♯**	**G**	**A**			**B**	**D**	

This is accompanied on the lower strings by the 'um cha cha' rhythm typical of waltzes, but this remains in the background as the strong melody conjures up a picture of 19th century ballrooms and swirling couples.

Activity 1   Musical pictures

Listen to track 43 Waltz

Does the music make the children think of a scene or picture as they listen? (To encourage their own responses, do not tell them the title.)

cont

Point out that music makes people respond in different ways, sometimes in thoughts of pictures or stories, sometimes creating a feeling or mood. Their interpretation may be quite different from the composer's intentions. Tell them the title, show them the waltz picture on page 53, and listen again. Does the music help them imagine a ballroom filled with dancing couples?

Activity 2   Composing a musical picture

Using instruments of one family, groups of children will choose a picture to describe in music by creating a matching mood.

What you will need
– a copy of the worksheet opposite for each group
– enlarged copies of each group's chosen picture
– a cassette recorder
– instruments divided by the children into families, eg

 **String**
guitars, violins, autoharps, home-made zithers (rubber bands stretched over open box)

 **Untuned wood/metal/skin**
castanets, wood blocks, claves, cymbals, guiro, bells, triangles, tambours

 **Wind**
recorder, whistles, panpipes, flutes, plastic tubes, bottles

 **Tuned wood/metal**
chime bars, gato drum, xylophone, glockenspiel, metallophone

What to do
• Give each group time to try out and refine their ideas, then let each group perform their piece to the class.

What to assess
What do the children think of or feel as they listen to each group's composition? (This may not correspond with the chosen picture, but there may be valid reasons for the children's feelings. What made them feel this way, eg 'the tinkly sounds made me feel cold'.)

Composing a musical picture

Work in groups.

1. Choose a picture and talk about the mood you want to give to your music, eg will it be exciting, frightening, joyful, energetic, tiring?

2. Choose a family of instruments which you think can describe this mood. Try out some ideas with your instruments.

3. Think about how you will organise your music:
• can you use your picture as a score, showing you when to play, or will it simply give you ideas?
• will you need to write anything down, or choose a conductor?
• will your music have a beat or will the sounds be played freely?
• when will it be loud or quiet, fast or slow, smooth or spiky, high or low?

4. Record and listen to your music as you work. Can you make it describe the mood of your picture more clearly. Can you hear all the sounds, or is the music sometimes too crowded?

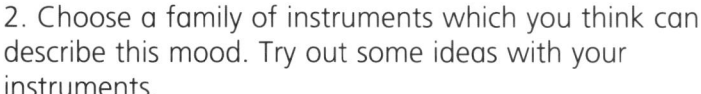

Listening links

What you need to know about the music

Scherzo from The 'trout' quintet
Composer: Franz Schubert (1797–1828)

This movement is the third of five; its title means 'playful'. Its tempo is indicated *presto* – very fast. The strongly rhythmical melody is introduced by all the instruments, then fragments are passed back and forth from strings to piano. The joyful mood is emphasised by the speed and the energetic rhythms.

Le rossignol
Composer: Franz Liszt (1811-86)

Liszt was a Hungarian pianist whose virtuoso playing led to the popularity of piano recitals across Western Europe in the 19th century. He was also a renowned composer and piano teacher, often composing pieces of great technical difficulty, which were innovative in exploring the sounds and textures of the piano. *Le rossignol* (nightingale) opens with rising patterns, then repeated notes at the top of the piano's range to imitate the song of the nightingale of the title. A long trill (adjacent notes alternated very quickly) and cascading, harp-like sounds lead into a slow, expressive, romantic melody. (*Answer to 3: acacacacdb*)

Sursum corda
Composer: Edward Elgar (1857–1934)

Sursum corda was composed in 1894 for a visit to Worcester Cathedral by the future King George V. Its Latin title means 'lift up your hearts' and the music is for strings, brass, timpani and organ. Listen for:
• a downward leap by the brass
• a swelling crescendo accompanied by timpani roll
• a slowly rising, expressive melody on the strings
• the brass returning with the solemn opening
• the development of the string melody.

19th century timpani

Track 44 — Scherzo from The 'trout' quintet

1. How would you describe the mood or feeling of this piece?

1.

2. Sometimes all the instruments play together. What happens in between?

2.

3. Can you label the five instruments in this picture? They all play in **The 'trout' quintet**?

3.

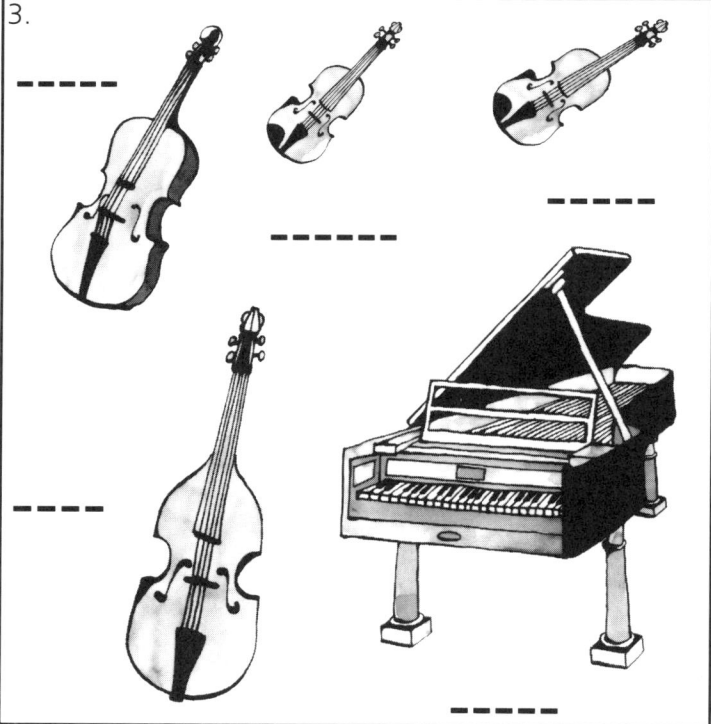

- - - - -

- - - - -

- - - - -

- - - - -

- - - - -

4. With a partner, have a musical conversation on percussion instruments. Take it in turns to play short rhythms. Keep a steady beat and try to pass the rhythms back and forth without stopping.

Track 45 — Le rossignol

1. What is the instrument you hear?

1. [_____]

2. What do you think this music describes?

2. [_____]

3. The composer uses several musical shapes in the first section before we hear the melody. Look at the pictures of the shapes – each has a letter. Write the letters in the box in the order you hear them. Careful! – they come more than once.

4. Now use the shapes and add more of your own to compose a birdsong piece for a tuned instrument (eg keyboard, recorder, violin or glockenspiel).

3. 4.

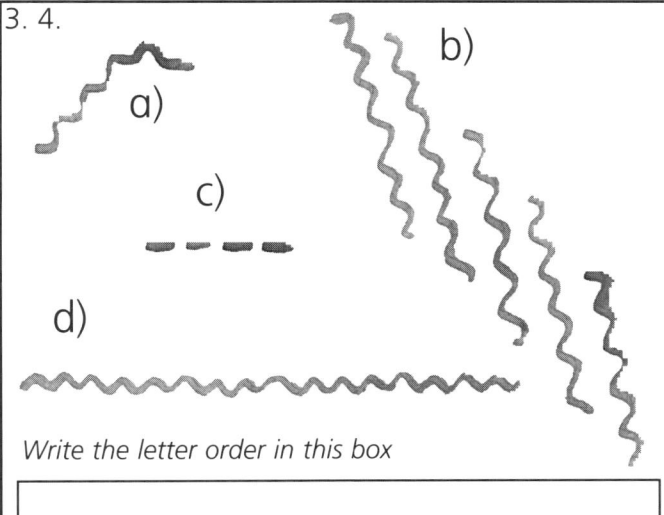

a)

b)

c)

d)

Write the letter order in this box

[_____]

Use this space to draw your new shapes and letter them

Write the letter order of your new piece in this box

[_____]

Track 46 — Sursum corda

1. What sort of occasion do you think this music was composed for?

1. [_____]

2. Why?

2. [_____]

3. One of the families of instruments is missing from this piece, but which one? Circle it in this picture.

4. Compose a short piece of music or song for a special occasion, eg
• a birthday
• your last day at primary school
• the death of a pet
• a trip on a rollercoaster.

3.

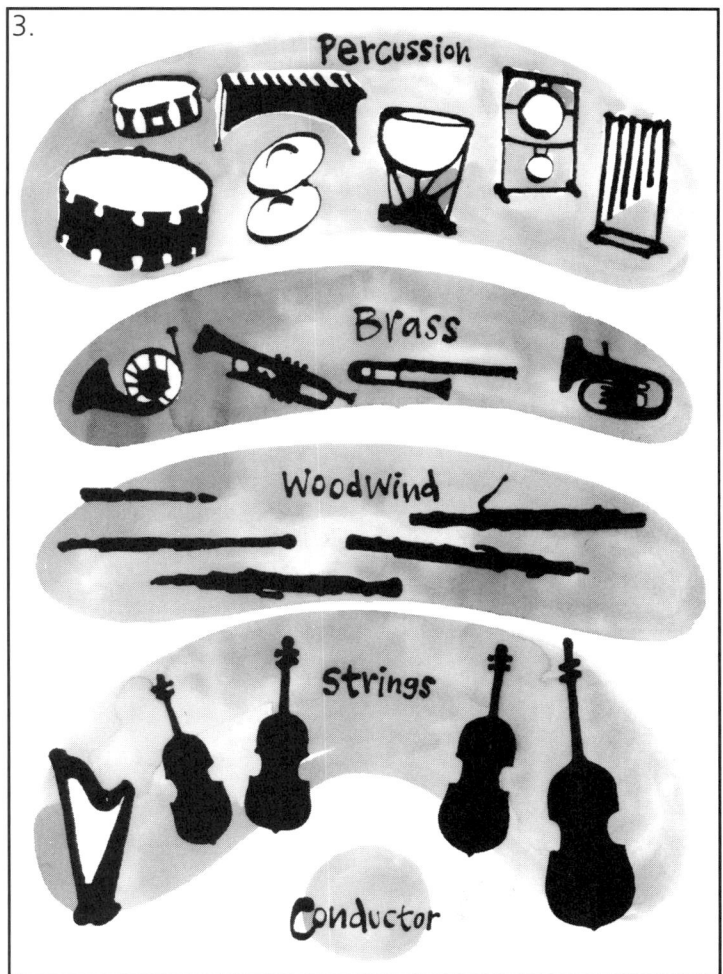

Percussion

Brass

Woodwind

Strings

Conductor

The 20th century has seen an explosion of different explorations in music, with many varied styles and influences emerging from the late 1800s onwards.

At the turn of the century, French Impressionists were experimenting with new ways of painting the effects of changing light, movement and colour in nature. French composers used changing timbres and chords to give musical impressions of similar subjects - clouds, rain, snow, sea.

Impressionist composers organised sounds in a new way – using subtly changing harmonies, free rhythms often sounding like improvisations, descriptive instrumental timbres and textures – almost as though they were painters themselves, using sounds like brush strokes.

Gnossienne no 3
by Erik Satie

This is the last of a set of three piano pieces, and is arranged here for orchestra. The title, coined by Satie, seems to refer to the ancient world of Knossos, and Satie's use of unusual scales gives the piece an unfamiliar and intriguing quality. His unconventional approach to composition was characteristic of the experimental mood amongst many composers at the beginning of the century.

American composers have developed their own distinctive music during the century, often influenced by popular American culture, especially blues and jazz.

Aaron Copland was keen to provide audiences with an 'American style' and many of his compositions contain entertaining references to American life.

Contemporary composers have an increasingly vast wealth of easily accessible music and instruments from other cultures to draw on for inspiration. Many composers fuse different styles and influences in their compositions to create exciting new sounds.

Fanfare for the common man
by Aaron Copland

This is an example of Copland's more serious output. Commissioned during World War II and dedicated to those involved, it is an impressively moving and optimistic tribute. It is played by brass instruments – trumpets and horns – and instruments of the percussion family, which throughout the century have been receiving more prominent roles in works of all kinds.

Today's composers write music for many different uses: for concerts; theme and background music for TV and film; music for dance, theatre and opera; pieces for special players or groups of musicians; and music for anniversaries, celebrations and state occasions.

Sextet
by Eleanor Alberga

From a suite of five dances, Dancing with the shadow. The first movement is a duet (for two players), the second a trio (for three) and so on to the sextet (for six players). The fast, syncopated rhythms and varied instrumental timbres reflect Alberga's richly diverse musical background.

Gnossienne no 3

What you need to know about the music

Composer: Erik Satie (1866–1925)

Satie began his musical education with a local organist who introduced him to medieval plainsong. At the age of thirteen he studied music at the Paris conservatoire but his teachers were not impressed with his skills. His compositions were often thought to be eccentric. They are littered with obscure instructions to the player: 'arm yourself with clairvoyance', 'open the head' appear on this piece.

His two sets of piano pieces, *Trois Gymnopedies* and *Trois Gnossiennes* (1890), seem to be dances inspired by ancient worlds: Greece and Knossos. This version of *Gnossienne no 3* has been arranged for orchestra.

Features of the music

• Simple step-by-step melodies are played by harp, flute, oboe and violin in turn while the body of the orchestra plays an accompaniment pattern.
• The melodies are based on three sets of notes (scales) which are unusual.
• These melodies move in two contrasting ways:
1. each note played then immediately repeated;
2. notes played one at a time in rising and falling waves.
• The accompaniment is a simple repeating rhythm using a limited number of chords based on the three scales.

Activity 1   Impressions

Listen to track 47 Gnossienne no 3

Ask the children for their impressions of the piece. They may like to move, paint or draw as they listen instead of describing their reactions in words.

Discuss their responses and how these link with the features in the music (described above).

Activity 2

scale 1

scale 2

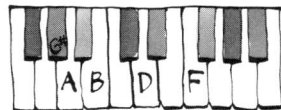

scale 3

Gnossienne scales

The children will become familiar with the sound of the notes of the scales which Satie uses in the piece, and will then create new scales of their own.

What you will need

– a keyboard, glockenspiel, or xylophone with the notes of scales 1, 2 and 3.

What to do

Familiarise the children with the unusual scales by giving them practice in singing the notes. Choose one child to come out and play a short pattern using the notes of scale 1. The rest of the class immediately sings back the pattern (to *la*). Continue with new patterns.

Repeat with scales 2 and 3 and different players.

What to do next

Let individual children invent their own five or six-note scales and compose simple melodies. First they will need to try out different groups of notes until they find a set they like. Ask them to write down their scales.

Listen to their melodies and compare the chosen sets of notes with each other.

What to assess

Have the children carefully chosen the notes of their scales and noticed the effect their choice has on melody? Do any of the scales remind the children of music they have heard before? (Some combinations may result in very familiar-sounding music – such as in the songs the children know; others may feel completely unfamiliar.)

Activity 3

high

middle

low

Gnossienne chords

The children will use their voices to build and become familiar with the three-note chords which Satie uses in Gnossienne no 3.

What you will need

– individual chime bars or three xylophones with these notes (see left).

What to do

Allocate the low notes of each chord to one child, the middle notes of each chord to a second child, and the high notes to a third. Number each set of notes, 1, 2, and 3.

Divide the rest of the class into three groups – low middle and high – and sit each group with their respective player.

Now try each of these techniques.

Chord building

Chord 1 – A, C E (track 48)

1. Low group. The tuned percussion child plays A continuously (repeatedly tapping the note). The other children in the group join in by continuously singing or humming the note, breathing as necessary.

2. Middle group. Play, sing and hum C continuously joining in with the low group.

3. High group. Play, sing and hum E continuously joining in with the low group. You should now be able to hear all three notes of the chord sounding at once.

Chord 2 – D F A, and Chord 3 – E G B (track 48)

Repeat the process, building the other two chords from low to high in the same way. When the children are confident at singing the three chords try building them from the top of the chord to the lowest notes.

low   middle   high

chord 1   low   middle   high

chord 2   low   middle   high

chord 3   high   middle   low

Chord changing

Choose a conductor. The conductor will hold up 1, 2 or 3 fingers to indicate which chord to play and sing. Having had enough practice in gradually building the chords one note at a time, the groups will be ready now to change quickly in response to the conductor. (An example of this can be heard on **track 49**.)

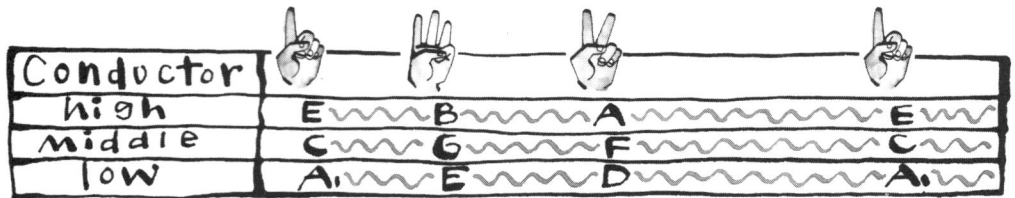

Conductor				
high	E	B	A	E
middle	C	G	F	C
low	A	E	D	A

Looking at major and minor chord shapes

Ask one child to play chord 1 on a keyboard. What do the others notice about the pattern of notes on the keyboard? (It is built on alternate white notes.)

Choose two more children to play chords 2 and 3. What do the children notice about these? (They are also built on alternate white notes.)

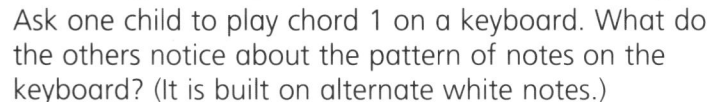

Now, play the same pattern starting on a different note – try C E G. Do the children notice any difference between the sound of this chord and the first three? (Some may say it sounds brighter.) Can the children *see* why there might be a difference in sound?

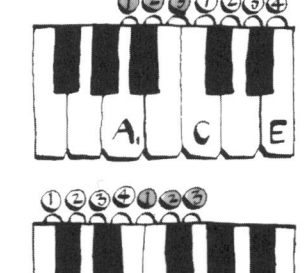

(Including black keys, count how many steps there are from one note of the chord to the next. ACE, DFA and EGB all have the same pattern of 3+4 steps; CEG is the other way round – 4+3.) The first three are called minor chords, the fourth is a major chord. Can the children build another major chord with the 4+3 shape?

Chord sequences

Working in pairs ask the children to compose a short piece made of a short sequence of chords 1, 2 and 3. They may choose to play all the chord notes at the same time, or find ways of arranging the chord notes in a pattern, eg (**track 50**):

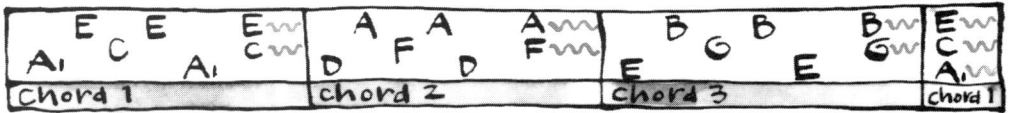

| Chord 1 | chord 2 | chord 3 | chord 1 |

Activity 4   *Satiesfied*

The children work in groups of four or more with Satie's chords and scales to create a new piece of music, which moves in a similar way to Satie's music.

What to assess

Are the children able to perform their pieces effectively, showing an ability to move smoothly from one chord to another, improvising within the given scales and devising and using a plan if necessary?

Listen to track 47 Gnossienne no 3

Before going on to Activity 3, use the plan below, which shows the structure of the beginning of the piece, to help the children recognise the features of Satie's composition. Ask them to indicate with hand signals the repeated note melodies and the wave shape melodies as they listen. Can they recognise when the repeated note melody begins on a new group of scale notes?

Scale 1		Scale 2		Scale 3			
harp: repeated note melody	flute and harp: repeated note melody again	oboe: repeated note melody	oboe: waves	harp: repeated note melody	harp and flute: repeated note melody	oboe: waves	flute: waves

Satiesfied

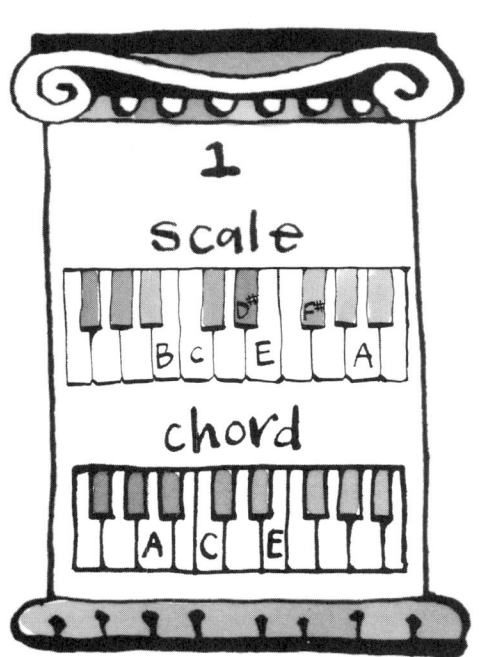

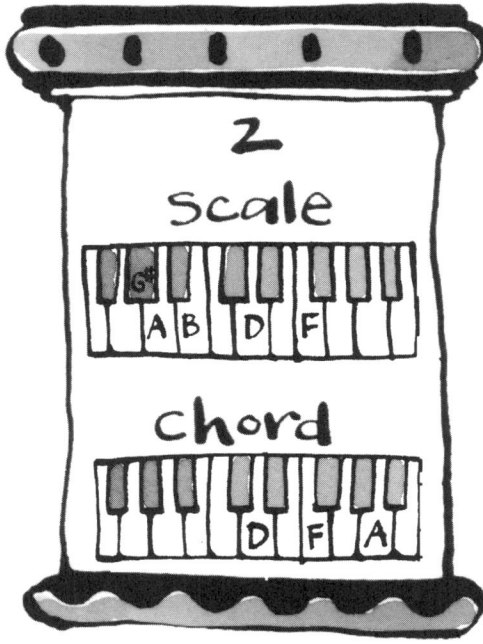

Work in a group of four or more.

What you will need for your group
– melody instruments with the notes for each of the scales – 1, 2, 3 above. A cassette recorder.
– tuned instruments for each chord.
(Share if you like.)

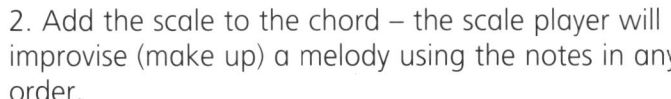

What to do
1. Choose one person to play scale 1. Everyone else will play chord 1. Decide how you will share out the three notes and how you will play them, eg overlapping to build up the chord, or all at once. Will you play repeating rhythms or long sounds?

2. Add the scale to the chord – the scale player will improvise (make up) a melody using the notes in any order.

3. Try out your ideas for the other two scales and chords with two more melody soloists.

4. Now decide how you will put your piece together using all three scales and chords. Play them in different orders and decide which you like. Recording your ideas on cassette as you work will help you to choose. How will you know when to change to a new chord and scale? How many times will you play each of them?

5. Practise and revise your piece until you are happy with it. You may need to write a plan of it. Record the final version and play it to the class.

Fanfare for the common man

What you need to know about the music

Composer: Aaron Copland (1900–1990)

The son of Russian Jews who emigrated to New York, Copland discovered as a child that he was interested in music and by the age of 21 had saved enough money to go to Paris to study composition. After returning to America in 1924 he composed many successful and popular works. He was keen to develop an American style and included jazz rhythms, folk song and square. dance melodies in his music.

Features of the music

Valveless trumpet

Fanfares are flourishes typically played on trumpets. They have been used for centuries to herald royal or military processions or celebrations. Trumpets were originally valveless and therefore restricted in the notes they could play – the characteristic melodic leaps of a fanfare were determined by this.

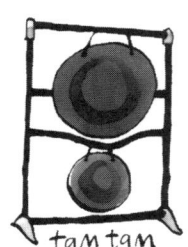

tam tam

Copland's fanfare (1942), was commissioned by the conductor of the Cincinnati Symphony Orchestra as a tribute to the Allied troops involved in World War II. Characteristically, Copland dedicated it to all the 'ordinary people' who win no fame or glory in battle. It is written for an orchestra of brass and percussion, and unlike most fanfares, has a slow, solemn mood.

Activity

Play and compose a fanfare

Pairs of children will play a short version of the fanfare (staff notation page 78), then compose their own.

Listen to track 51 Fanfare for the common man

Look at the graphic score of the opening on page 71 as you listen, noticing:
• repetition of three solemn drum beats with tam tam (large gong) on the first of each three • trumpets playing leaping phrases in unison • repeats of the percussion • trumpets' melody returning with horns playing below.

Play and compose a fanfare

Work in pairs and teach yourselves how to play this version of Copland's fanfare. (It is split into three to make it easier to practise.)

Use any instrument with these notes:

player 1

player 2

Player 1

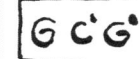  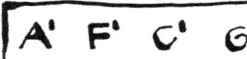

Player 1 (top) and player 2

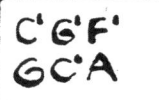 

Now work with another pair to add the percussion

A new fanfare

Compose a new fanfare. Decide whether to make up a solemn or joyful fanfare, then use these combinations of notes in any order.

Add percussion

Join with another pair and add percussion.
Decide how many times you will play the fanfares and percussion patterns.

Photocopiable worksheet

Fanfare for the common man (opening)

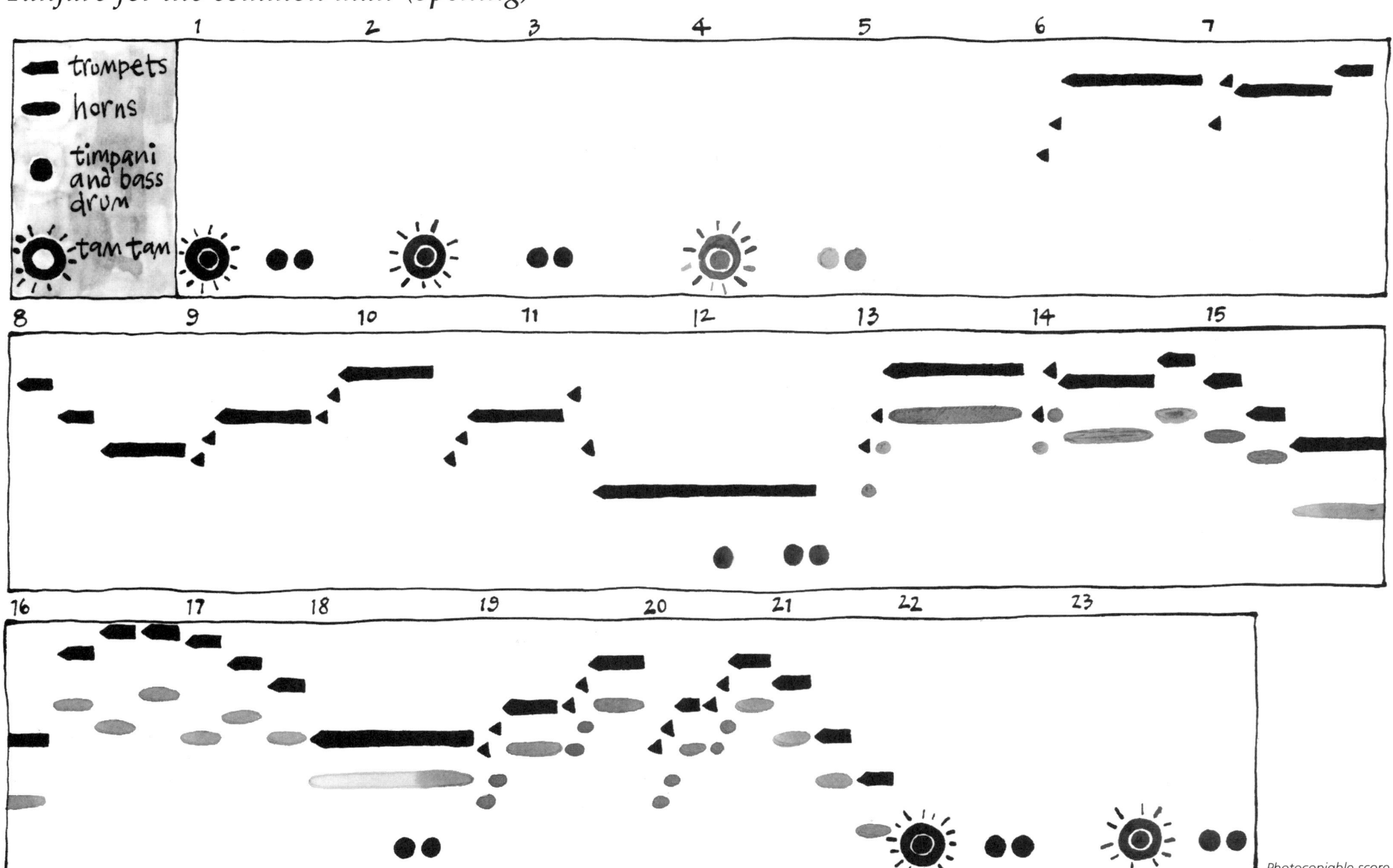

Photocopiable score

Sextet from Dancing with the shadow

What you need to know about the music

Composer: Eleanor Alberga (b 1949)

Alberga was born in Jamaica and trained in classical music at the Royal Academy of Music in London. She has experience as a member of the 'Jamaican folk singers' and an African dance company. She began composing for the London Contemporary Dance Theatre, has written film scores and a musical setting of Roald Dahl's *Snow white and the seven dwarfs*.

Features of the music

This piece is the final movement from the music for a set of five dances. It is scored for sextet (six players) playing flute, clarinet, violin, cello, piano and a range of percussion instruments.

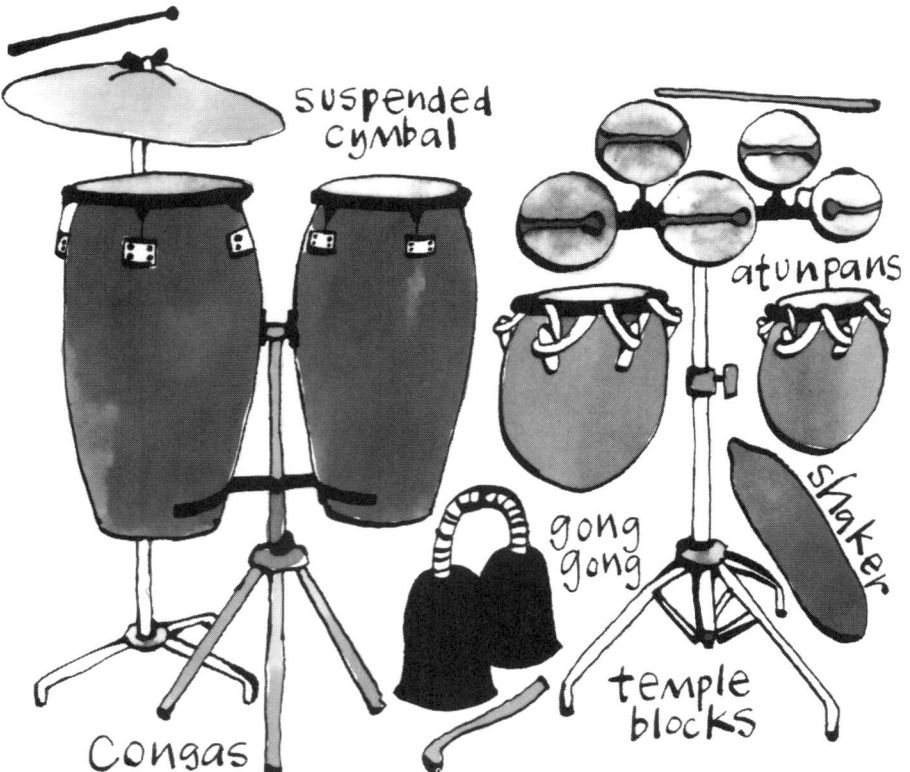

suspended cymbal

atunpans

gong gong

shaker

temple blocks

Congas

Alberga uses the different timbres of the instruments (eg the congas are played with stick against side as well as by hands on skin). Short solo sections feature individual instruments as in jazz improvisations. Calmer, slower sections are heard but soon give way to the busy and exhilarating mood of the whole piece.

Activity   Percussion sextet

The children will work in groups of six to make a composition which contrasts short sounds in a fast tempo with long sounds in a slow tempo. One child conducts, and devises an aural or visual signal to indicate the beginning of each section.

Listen to track 52 Sextet from Dancing with the shadow

The children will need to listen more than once to answer the questions below. Timings (eg 47") will help you to find the relevant part of the recording. The piece starts with a crescendo (increase in volume) played by two percussion instruments setting a fast, exciting beat. The whole ensemble enters with off-beat rhythms. Individual instruments are featured in short solos and duets in between sections involving the whole group.

Questions you might ask
*Can you identify the instruments as they are featured? (Piano – 35";
clarinet – 47"; flute and clarinet together – 1.05"; piano and percussion –
1'36"; percussion solo – 1'44".)*
*Do you recognise any instruments you have used in school? (eg shaker,
cymbal, woodblock/temple block ...)*
*Do you notice any changes in the mood during this piece? (It starts in a
lively, energetic mood, then there are some calm slower, quieter sections.)*
*Can you describe the sound of the clarinet when it first appears? (It plays
some very high notes. It sounds smooth as it jumps up and down from high
to lower notes – 47".)*
*Can you find some smooth, gentle sounds in this piece and describe them.
(Flute plays long notes immediately after the clarinet solo – 58". The violin,
clarinet and flute play up and down waves – 1'27". The flute and clarinet
play long, smooth notes – 2'.)*

Percussion sextet

Work in groups of six.

Fast section – short sounds

What you will need

A variety of percussion instruments, eg drums, shakers, claves.

What to do

• Play each line separately (you can hear them on **track 53**), repeating it several times without a break and keeping a steady beat. Player 1 counts the beat.

1	2	3	4	5	6	7	8

1	2	3	4	5	6	7	8
🪘	🪘	🪘	🪘	🪘	🪘	🪘	🪘
➤	➤	➤	➤	➤	➤	➤	➤
🪇			🪇				
					▬	▬	▬
🔨🔨	🔨🔨	🔨🔨	🔨🔨	🔨🔨	🔨		

Next, try playing two or more lines together, practising until you can play them with a quick, steady beat. Instead of counting aloud, player 1 now conducts the beat silently.

Now make up your own rhythms. Each choose your own numbers to play on – or between – and draw them on the empty grid opposite. Practise repeating each line separately then combine lines. Make a note of the order of the combinations like this:

1st 8 counts	2nd 8 counts	3rd 8 counts	4th 8 counts
Jo and Ayshe	Jo, Ayshe Siva	All	Carlie and Tim

Make up three or four more fast sections in this way.

Slow section – long sounds

What you will need

Cymbals, triangle, recorder, chime bar – instruments which can make long sounds.

Layer your long sounds, one on top of another. Decide which combinations you like best.

Make a note of the order in which you enter. Player 1 conducts. **Track 54** gives you this example:

> 1st slow section
> Jo
> Tim   Siva   Ayshe   Jo
>   Carlie   All

Now put together the whole piece of music.
• How many different fast sections will you play?
• How many slow sections?
• What will be the signal to change to a new section?

Listening links

What you need to know about the music

La nuit

Composer: Erik Satie (1866–1925)

This piece is from a ballet, 'Les aventures de Mercure' (1924), composed during a period when Satie was collaborating with Jean Cocteau and Pablo Picasso. Together with the choreographer Leonide Massine they produced several ballets which experimented with Cubist ideas. Set and costume designs were by Picasso and this ballet featured three-dimensional poses set to brief pieces of music. The opening sets an atmosphere of night with dark timbres, low pitches and quiet, slow murmurs.

Konzertmusik for brass and strings

Composer: Paul Hindemith (1895–1963)

This is one of a group of pieces, composed in 1931, which Hindemith wrote for different combinations of instruments. He himself was able to play every orchestral instrument, although his main instrument was viola. For this piece he used a string quartet (two violins, viola and cello), four horns, four trumpets, three trombones and a tuba. The second section, heard here, begins with a strong, rising, three-note melody, contrasted with fast, running melodies on the strings. The instruments take turns to play as if chasing one an other.

Paris fanfare

Composer: Paul Patterson (b 1947)

This fanfare was composed for the state opening of the Channel Tunnel in 1994. It was played on the arrival at Waterloo of Queen Elizabeth II and was broadcast on international television. Patterson combined the opening of the *Marseillaise* with *Rule Britannia* in a triumphant and impressive flourish of brass instruments to symbolise the meeting of the two countries.

Track 55

class

La nuit (The night)

Work as a class to make a short piece of music describing night.

Use the notes on the chart to make a background of sounds. Choose the lowest, darkest-sounding instruments you can find for this. Play slowly and quietly. Repeat the sounds as many times as you want.

Now think of some other night sounds for instruments or voices to make – a swooping bat, a hooting owl, snuffling hedgehog. Think about the atmosphere you want to create – is it calm, peaceful, spooky, mysterious?

Try out your ideas. Choose the ones you want to use, draw them and stick them on to the picture above.

Record your music and listen to the effects. Keep changing them until you are happy with them.

Now listen to **La nuit**. Satie uses a similar background. What other sounds does he add?
What atmosphere do you think he creates?

Photocopiable worksheet

Track 56 — Konzertmusik

Work in small groups. You will need one instrument each, eg

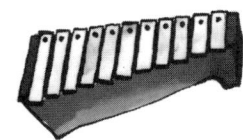

1. Listen to the music. Which two instrument families are playing?

2. Describe or draw the first three sounds you hear.

3. After the first three sounds, notice that the violin plays very fast, lively, running melodies. Draw the shape of these running patterns.

4. Use these two ideas to compose a short copying piece for your instruments.

three short notes • fast running melodies

6. Draw a plan of your music to show the order in which the instruments join in.

Track 57 — Paris fanfare

Work on your own. You will need one tuned instrument

1. Ask a teacher or another adult to sing you the opening of *Rule Britannia* and *The Marseillaise*.

2. Listen to **Paris fanfare**. This fanfare was composed in 1994 for the Queen's arrival at Waterloo station to celebrate the opening of the Channel Tunnel. Do you recognise the tunes the composer uses? Why do you think the composer has used these two tunes?

3. Imagine there is life on Mars and you are visiting the planet. When you arrive, the Martians welcome you by playing a fanfare of their national music. It is not like anything you have heard on earth!

Make up a Martian melody on your tuned instrument. You may like to make up some words in Martian language to sing with your tune.

Staff notation

Eno sagrado en Vigo (page 12)

E - no sa - gra -do en Vi - go

Bey - la - va cor -po ve - li - do. Am -or ei.

Aj ondas que eu vin veer (page 12)

Aj on - das que eu vin veer,

se me sa - be - re - des di - zer

por - que tar - da me - u a -

- mi - go sen min?

Danse royale (page 15)

Sing a song – melody and first relay (page 19)

Sing a song to ce - le - brate at Christ- mas time.

Sing a song to ce - le - brate at Christ- mas time

Martin said to his man (page 23)

Mar - tin said to his man, *Fie, man, fie!*

Mar - tin said to his man, *Who's the fool now?*

Mar - tin said to his man, *'Fill thou the cup and I the can.'*

Thou hast well drunk - en man, Who's the fool now?

Thou hast well drunk - en man, Who's the fool now?

Mistress Winter's jump (page 25)

Chiacona (page 32)

Canzona super entrada aechiopicam (page 38)

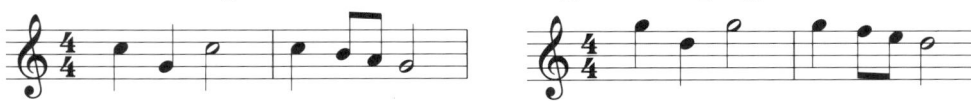

A Christmas carol – bass line (page 47)

A Christmas carol (page 47)

Let an an-them of_ praise and a_ ca-rol of joy Each tongue and each_ heart in sweet_ con-cert em-ploy: This day sprung at Beth-l'em a plant of re- -nown, And Christ_ to_ re-deem us a-ban-doned a_ crown.

Ein Mädchen oder Weibchen (page 49)

Andante

O mai-den come to join___ me, be Pa-pa-ge-no's wife, A tur-tle dove be-side me___ that's___ all I ask___ of___ life! Each

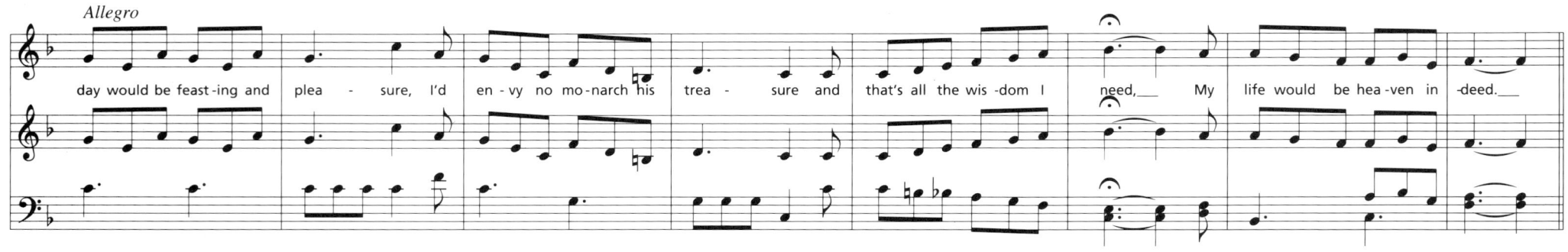

Allegro

day would be feast-ing and plea - sure, I'd en-vy no mo-narch his trea - sure and that's all the wis-dom I need,___ My life would be hea-ven in -deed.___

Polka ostinato (page 59)

Fanfare for the common man – player 1 (page 70)

Polka duet melodies (page 59)

Fanfare for the common man – players 1 and 2

Acknowledgements

The copyright recordings listed below have been used by permission of

hyperion

PO Box 25, London SE9 1AX Tel 0181 294 1166
Fax 0181 294 1161 Email: info@hyperion-records.co.uk

Columba aspexit (English translation by Christopher Page) and **O viridissima virga** from *A feather on the breath of God*, performed by *Gothic Voices* with Emma Kirkby. Catalogue number **66039**.

Estampie royal (no 4), **Danse royale** (no 2), **Eno sagrado en Vigo** and **Aj ondas que eu vin veer** (both English translations by Stephen Haynes) from *Bella Domna*, performed by *Sinfonye* with Maria Kiek (voice), directed by Stevie Wishart. Cat no **66283**.

Mistress Winter's jump and **Suzanna** from *Consort music by John Dowland*, performed by *Extempore String Ensemble* directed by Weigand. Cat no **66010**.

Pueri concinite from *Christmas music from Medieval and Renaissance Europe*, performed by *The Sixteen* directed by Harry Christophers. Cat no **66263**.

Martin said to his man and **Packington's pound** from *How the world wags*, performed by *The City Waites*. Cat no **66008**.

In nomine from *For His Majesty's Sagbutts and Cornetts* performed by *His Majesty's Sagbutts and Cornetts*. Cat no **66894**.

Chiacona and **Canzona super entrada aechiopicam** (Canzona super cantionem gallicam 'Est-ce mars?') from *His Majesty's Sagbutts and Cornetts Grand Tour*, performed by *His Majesty's Sagbutts and Cornetts*. Cat no **66847**.

Recorder Concerto (Concerto in A minor) from *Vivaldi Recorder Concertos*, performed by Peter Holtslag and *The Parley of Instruments*. Cat no **66328**.

Chorus from The 'hunt' cantata (Cantata 208) from *Bach Hunt Cantata*, performed by *The Parley of Instruments* directed by Roy Goodman. Cat no **66169**.

The 'hen' symphony (Symphony no 83 in g minor) from *Symphonies of Haydn*, performed by *The Hanover Band* directed by Roy Goodman. Cat no **66527**.

A Christmas carol (Let an anthem of praise) from *While shepherds watched*, performed by *Psalmody* and *The Parley of Instruments* directed by Peter Holman. Cat no **66924**.

Variations on 'Ein Mädchen oder Weibchen' from *Beethoven cello sonatas*, performed by Anthony Pleeth and Melvyn Tan. Cat no **22004**.

The 'trout' quintet (Quintet in A major, D667) from *Schubert's Trout Quintet*, performed by *The Schubert Ensemble* of London. Cat no **22008**.

Polka and **Le Rossignol** from *Liszt Arabesques*, performed by Howard. Cat no **66984**.

Sursum corda, **Paris Fanfare** and **Konzertmusk** (op 50) from *The Royal Eurostar and other brass music*, performed by *London Brass Virtuosi* and *The Philharmonic Orchestra* directed by Honeyball. Cat no **66870**.

Fanfare for the common man from *Music for Brass and Percussion*, performed by *London Brass Virtuosi* directed by Honeyball. Cat no **66189**.

Gnossienne no 3 and **La nuit** (from 'Mercure') from *Satie's Theatre Music*, performed by *New London Orchestra* directed by Ron Corp. Cat no **66365**.

In addition to the recordings listed above the following copyright recordings have been included by kind permission of these copyright holders:

Sextet from 'Dancing with the shadow' by Eleanor Alberga from *British Women Composers – Vol 2* released by **Lontano Records**, 28 Commercial Street, London E1 6LS. Cat no **LNT 103**.

Ein Mädchen oder Weibchen from *Die Zauberflöte* performed by *Drottingholm Concert Theatre* directed by Östman © PolyGram. Cat no Decca Classics **440 085–2**.

Waltz from *Serenade for Strings* performed by *Netherlands Symphony Orchestra* directed by Zinman © PolyGram. Cat no Philips Classics **438 748–2**.

We are also grateful to the following copyright owners for their permission to include copyright music recordings, notation and text:

Fanfare for the common man by Aaron Copland Copyright 1944 by the Aaron Copland Fund for Music, Inc. Copyright renewed. Boosey & Hawkes, Inc. Sole licensee. Reproduced by permission of Boosey & Hawkes Music Publishers Ltd.

O maiden come to join me (translation by Andrew Porter of the first verse of Ein Mädchen oder Weibchen) © Faber Music Ltd.

Translations of **Columba aspexit**, **Eno sagrado en Vigo** and **Aj ondas que eu vin veer** © Hyperion.

All other recordings produced by A & C Black:

Sonata for harpsichord, performed by Timothy Roberts; **The candle**, **Melody of Martin said to his man**, **Melody of A Christmas carol**, **Melody of O maiden come to join me**, all performed by Rosamund Chadwick; **Chiacona ground bass and decorations** performed by Timothy Roberts (harpsichord) and Jeremy West (cornett). Track announcements by Jonathan Trueman. All other supplementary recordings performed by Helen MacGregor and Stephen Chadwick. © A & C Black.

Index

Bold page numbers indicate where an explanation or illustration may be found. Very frequently used terms are described in the glossary opposite.

acoustics in churches 16
Alberga, Eleanor 65, **72**
Albigensian Crusades 10
Alwood, Richard 26
antiphony 16 18
aria 41, 48
Ashworth, Caleb 41, **46**
atunpans **72**

Bach, Johann Sebastian 38
bagpipes 50
baroque 28
bass viol 24
bass sackbut 30
bass clarinet 52
bassoon – in baroque orchestra 29; in *The hunt cantata* 38; in classical orchestra 40; in *The hen symphony* 42; in *A Christmas carol* 46
Beethoven, Ludwig van 50
binary 34, 35
blues 65
Borodin, Alexander 53 58
brass family 29, 62, 63, 65, 70, 74

cantata 29, 38
Cantigas de amigo 12
canzona 38
Catholics 24
cello (violincello) in *Recorder concerto* 36; in *The 'trout' quintet* 52, 54-7; in *Sextet* 72
chamber organ 26 38
chamber orchestra 29
chamber concerto 36
chanson de femmes 14
chest of viols 17
Christianity 4
clarinet 40; in *Sextet* 72
coda 42, 44
Codax, Martin 12
concerto grosso 29
concerto – in baroque 29
congas 72
consort 17; of lutes 26; of recorders 17; of viols 17

Copland, Aaron 65 70
cornett 30, 38
crusaders 16

de Fournival, Richart 14
decorations 24, 30, 32, 54
Deuteromelia 22
development 42, 44
devotional song 4, 6
double dance step 24
double bass – in *The 'trout' quintet* 52, 54-7
Dowland, John 17 **24**
drone 6, 12, 14, 50
d'Arrezzo, Guido 4

Elgar, Edward 62
encore 53
estampie 10
exposition 42, 44

fanfare 70 74-75
figured bass 29
first subject 42
flute 40; in *The hen symphony* 42; in *Gnossienne no 3* 66; in *Sextet* 72
fortepiano 48
frame drum 10

glissando 48
glockenspiel 41, 48
gong gong 72
ground bass 28, 30
guitar – in renaissance 24

hall in Tudor times 17
Handl, Jacob 16, 18
harp – in medieval music 12, 14; in *Gnossienne no 3* 66
harpsichord 28; in *Chiacona* 30; in *Harpsichord sonata* 34; in *Recorder concerto* 36; in *The hunt cantata* 38; in *Pastorale* 50
Haydn, Joseph 40, 42, 50
Hellendaal, Pieter 50
Henry VIII 17
Hildegard of Bingen 4, 6
Hindemith, Paul 74
homophony 18
horn in *The hunt cantata* 38; in *The 'hen' symphony* 42; in *Fanfare for the common man* 70; in *Konzertmuzik* 74

imitation 38
impressionists **64**

jazz 65

link 44
Lizt, Franz 53, 58, **62**
lute 24, 26

Magic Flute, The 48
major and minor chord shapes 68
major and minor keys 28, 34
mandolin 29
mandora 24
medieval fiddle 10, 14
medieval 4-5
melisma 6, 12
Merula, Tarquinio 28, 30
minstrels 5
minstrels' gallery 17
modes 5, 28
monasteries 4
Mozart, Wolfgang Amadeus 41, 48
Muslims and influence on medieval European music 10

Non-conformists 41

oboe – in baroque orchestra 29; in *The hunt cantata* 38; in classical orchestra 40; in *The 'hen' symphony* 42; in *Gnossienne no 3* 66
orchestra – baroque 29; classical 40; romantic 52
organ 48
ostinato 58

Papageno 41, 48
percussion family 63, 65
percussion – in *Fanfare for the common man* 70; in *Sextet* 72
piano 52-53; in *The 'trout' quintet* 54–57; in *Polka* 58-59; in *Le Rossignol* 62; in *Gnossienne no 3* 64; in *Sextet* 72
piccolo 52
plainsong (plainchant) – medieval 4; renaissance 26; and Satie 66
polka 53
polyphony 16, 18
Protestants 24

quintet 52, 54-57

Ravenscroft, Thomas 16, 22
recapitulation 42, 44
recorder 29; treble recorder in *Recorder concerto* 36, 38;
Reformation 29
reverence 24-25
Rimsky-Korsakov 53
Roman Empire 4
romantic 52-53

sackbut 30; in *Chiacona* 30; in *Canzona* 38
Satie, Eric 64, 66, 74
scale 28, 30
Scarlatti, Domenico 28, 34
Scheidt, Samuel 38
scherzo 62
Schubert, Franz 52, 54
sextet 65, 72
shaker 72
shawm 26
simple dance step 24
soirée 52
solo concerto 29
sonata form 40 42
sonata 28, 34
staff notation 4

stave 4
string quartet 52 74
strings – in baroque orchestra 29; in *Recorder concerto* 36, 38; in *The hen symphony* 42, 50 in *Pastorale* 50; in *Konzertmuzik* 74; in *Waltz* 60; in *Sursum corda* 62 63
subject, first and second 42, 44
suspended cymbal 72
symphony (hurdy gurdy) 6, 14
symphony (piece of music 40

tam tam 70
Tchaikovsky, Peter Ilyich 53, 60
temple blocks 72
theorbo (bass lute) 26
timpani 62
treble recorder 36
tricks in dances 17, 24
trill 34 54
trombone 74
troubadour 5
trouvère 5, 14
trumpet – in *Fanfare for the common man* 70; in *Konzertmuzik* 74; in *Paris Fanfare* 74
tuba 52

Tudors 17

valveless trumpet 70
variations 50, 52, 54-57
viol consort 17
viola – in *The 'trout' quintet* 52, 54-57
violin – medieval 10, 14; renaissance 24; baroque 29; concertos 29, 50; in *Recorder concerto* 36; in *Pastorale* 50; in *The 'trout' quinet* 52, 54-57; in *Gnossienne no 3* 66; in *Sextet* 72
violin family 29
Vivaldi, Antonio 29, 36, 38
voices - in medieval 4-6, 12, 14; in renaissance 16, 18, 22; in baroque 29, 38; in classical music 41, 46

waltz 53
woodwind family – in baroque orchestra 29; in classical orchestra 40; in *The hen symphony* 42; in *Pastorale* 50

First published 1998
by A & C Black (Publishers) Ltd
35 Bedford Row, London WC1R 4JH

Text © Helen MacGregor
Recording compilation © A & C Black
Illustrations © Alison Dexter
Cover illustration © Jane Tattersfield
Series design by Dorothy Moir
Editing and layout by Sheena Roberts
Supplementary recordings produced by Stephen Chadwick
Post-production by Simon Kahn
Music setting by Ana Sanderson
Origination of illustrations by Create Publishing Services, Bath

Printed in Great Britain
by St Edmundsbury Press,
Bury St Edmunds